Chapter One: The Hidden Manuscripts

Eliza opened the door to the study and entered,and paused, allowing her eyes to sweep over the room that stretched before her like a glimpse into another time. The walls were lined with heavy bookshelves, their dark wood polished to a deep sheen, while a rich tapestry of scents—aged leather, old paper, and something faintly sweet and earthy—drifted toward her. She flicked a switch on the wall, and the room filled with a soft, golden glow. The wall sconces, designed to look like old candles in holders, cast a warm light that flickered gently, adding an air of mystery to the scene.

Her iPhone's dim screen was a sharp contrast to this old-world ambiance. She placed it on the large oak desk, its sleek, modern form jarring against the aged wood. She hesitated, then switched it off, allowing the room's ambient glow to envelop her fully. There was something almost sacrilegious,about relying on technology here, in this room steeped in history.

The Manor house near Salisbury in Wiltshire, once the property of a distant branch of the Boleyn family, was now under the care of close friends who had offered her the chance to explore its hidden treasures while they were away on holiday. Eliza had eagerly accepted the thought of delving into centuries-old manuscripts, filling her with anticipation. It was a rare opportunity for any historian, and she intended to make the most of her solitude here.

The shelves were crammed with books, their spines cracked and faded, whispering of forgotten knowledge. Piles of manuscripts lay scattered across a long table, some bound in leather, others mere stacks of yellowed paper, curling at the edges. Eliza moved to the desk, her fingers brushing over the grain of the wood on the surface. She could almost feel the weight of history pressing down around her, the silent stories waiting to be uncovered.

She turned on a small desk lamp, its light pooling softly over the documents she had set aside for the evening. Her fingers tingled as she touched the ancient vellum, the inked letters forming words in languages she couldn't quite decipher. Each document seemed to pulse with a life of its own, secrets just beyond her reach. The atmosphere was electric, as if the room itself held its breath, waiting.

This particular manuscript was ancient, its leather cover cracked and worn by centuries of handling. The pages, yellowed with age, were brittle to the touch, the edges frayed from countless fingers that had turned them before her. The smell of old parchment filled the air, rich with the musty scent of time. Dust specks danced in the dim light as Eliza carefully opened the heavy book,the creaking spine groaning under its weight.

Nestled deep within the pages, hidden between the delicate sheets, was a small bundle wrapped in a faded, once vibrant cloth. The fabric had dulled over the years, now a patchwork of browns and ochres, but it had been folded with precision, almost reverence. Eliza's fingers trembled as she peeled back the cloth, revealing a locket,a silver oval, tarnished and cold. Its surface was engraved with intricate patterns and symbols , swirling designs that seemed almost too delicate for the roughness of the metal.

Beneath the locket, resting at the bottom of the bundle, was a parchment. It was brittle,its edges crumbling as Eliza lifted it gently. The ink was faded, but the words were still legible, written in an ancient hand that seemed familiar, yet foreign like a Masonic ritual she had read about in other books. The letters were bold, looping with care, the script resembling the ceremonial markings of some long-forgotten rite. The parchment held a sense of gravity, a weight that pressed down upon Eliza's chest as she read the first few lines.

The words on the page felt like a chant, a summoning, their meaning cryptic.

"In the shadow of time's ever-turning wheel, the bearer shall pass unseen. Mark the silver with care, for it is the key to all that was and all that will be"

Eliza's heart raced as the parchment seemed to pulse in her hand, the words,the key to all that was and all that will be, drawing her deeper into their mystery, the locket almost calling to her, as if waiting to be unlocked.

The symbols and patterns did indeed,appear to shift under the gentle light, their shapes twisting as if alive. Eliza's heart pounded in her chest, a mixture of fascination and unease washing over her. She reached out tentatively, her fingertips brushing the locket's surface. It was warm, almost alive,and the sensation seemed to travel up her arm, sending a ripple of energy through her.

Her hand then hovered over the silver locket, her fingers trembling slightly as she felt an invisible force drawing her in. She glanced around, half expecting to see someone watching her, but she was alone. Alone, yet not entirely. There was a presence in the room, a silent witness to her discovery.
The manuscripts on the desk seemed to rustle softly, as if stirred by a breeze that wasn't there. Eliza drew in a sharp breath, her pulse racing. She was no longer just a historian sifting through old papers,she felt she was connected to something far greater,something that transcended time and place.

Eliza picked it up and gazed at the beautiful locket in her hand, its very being, glowing faintly under the soft light. She felt compelled to read the words again on the parchment, to understand their meaning and the words seemed to echo in the quiet room, their sound wrapping around her like a tangible presence. The air felt thick, almost alive, as if the very fabric of reality was shifting. Eliza's fingers tightened around the locket, a sense of anticipation thrumming through her veins. She had never believed in the supernatural, not really. And yet, standing here, surrounded by ancient books and the weight of history, she felt the barriers of time and reality thinning, as if something—or someone—were reaching out to her from across the centuries.

The room seemed to darken at the edges of her vision, narrowing until only the locket existed, its surface glowing in her hand, softly in the lamplight. She could feel its energy surrounding her, drawing her closer, urging her to uncover its secrets.
She bent closer, the light casting her shadow over the parchment . The words were unlike anything she had seen before, an archaic script that seemed to ripple and pulse, the letters curling like tendrils. As she stared, the symbols on the locket seemed to shift, their meanings whispering at the edge of her understanding. She felt the urge to speak the words aloud, to bring them to life.
Her voice was a mere whisper as she read the lines again,and again feeling them vibrate through her, resonating with the energy that seemed to pulse from the locket:

The room seemed to hum softly, the sound resonating in her bones, growing stronger with each passing second. She could feel the locket's energy reaching out, like a magnetic field, pulling her closer, as if the object had been waiting for her, calling her to uncover its secrets.
A surge of energy pulsed through her hand,filling her with a strange, exhilarating sensation. It was as if the silver locket had unlocked a part of her, a doorway into a world she had only glimpsed in books and dreams. She could hardly breathe, her mind swirling with possibilities.
The light from the silver locket really flared, bright and blinding. Eliza gasped,and tried to put the locket down on the desk, but it was too late. The world around her

dissolved in a flash of brilliance, and she felt herself being pulled through the very fabric of reality. There was a moment of dizzying weightlessness, a sensation of falling through endless space.

And then, just as abruptly as it had begun, it was over.

Her heart still racing, Eliza tried to get herself up, her hands trembling. She looked around in confusion. The room she was in now was elegant and richly furnished, nothing like the study she had just been in. Heavy tapestries adorned the walls, depicting scenes of hunts and courtly life. A large fireplace dominated one wall, its embers glowing softly, casting flickering shadows across the intricately woven carpets and the dark wooden furniture.

Where was she?

Stumbling to her feet, Eliza moved to the door and peered out. Her breath caught in her throat as she saw people bustling about in clothing straight out of the 16th century. Women in long gowns of deep blues and rich crimson hues, their coifs neatly pinned, and men in doublets of red and gold, their hose stretched taut against muscular legs, feathers bobbing atop their hats with each animated gesture. Their faces were flushed with life and conversation, laughter mingling with the clatter of wooden heels on the stone floor.

She turned back to the room, her gaze falling on her own attire. Gone were her black trousers and sweater; in their place was a gown of sumptuous green, its fabric heavy and luxurious. The dress clung to her bodice and flared out into a wide skirt, the hem brushing against her ankles. A delicate lace coif adorned her head, its intricate patterns framing her face. Her hair, which had been in a casual ponytail moments before, was now arranged in an elegant braided style, tucked neatly beneath the coif. Panic surged. This had to be a dream—a vivid, terrifying dream. She pinched her arm, hard. The sharp pain made her gasp. Not a dream.

A sudden realisation struck her like a blow: the locket,the incantation—she had somehow travelled back in time. Heart pounding,Eliza forced herself to take a deep breath. She couldn't afford to panic, not now. She needed to think, to find out when and where she was. And most importantly, she needed to figure out how to get back. She started looking for the locket which had fell out of hand,her gaze suddenly falling onto her left hand. There, glinting softly in the dim light, was a ring. A delicate band of silver encircled her finger, set with a tiny small, shimmering stone.

Eliza's breath caught. She lifted her hand closer, and her heart skipped a beat as she saw the faint etchings along the band. The words,she read were, in an elegant, flowing script:
Tempus vincit omnia- Time conquers all

The ring was exquisitely beautiful and twisting it nervously on her finger, half-expecting it to vanish to leave her standing there with no proof that this was anything more than a hallucination. But it remained solid, the ring catching the light with a subtle, almost imperceptible glow. It felt warm against her skin, the metal cool and smooth and the locket,that she retrieved from the floor,was now safe in her hand. Whatever power it had held seemed to be gone, leaving her stranded in a world that was both familiar and utterly alien.

"Keep calm," she whispered to herself. "You're an historian. You can handle this."

But even as she said the words, doubt gnawed at her. This wasn't like studying an old text or deciphering ancient symbols from the safety of a library. She was here, in the past, surrounded by people who would consider her either mad or worse if they knew the truth. She swallowed hard, the taste of fear bitter on her tongue. She walked over to the ornate chair, its high back carved with intricate patterns, and sat down heavily, her mind racing..

What did she know about this period?

What could she remember from her books that would help her navigate this strange new world?

Hampton Court Palace,she thought suddenly,her heart leaping with hope. The grandeur of the setting, the distinctive clothing—it had to be. But which year? Which moment in history had she stumbled into? Eliza squeezed the locket in her hand,willing it to react,to give her some sign,some way back. But it remained cold and lifeless,mocking her desperation. She took another deep breath, forcing herself to focus. If she really was at Hampton Court Palace,she needed to keep her wits about her. One wrong move, one careless word, and she could find herself in serious danger.

Rising again,she moved to the door and peered out, watching the bustling figures. They seemed so real,so vivid,each movement and sound intensifying her sense of dislocation. This wasn't a reenactment, wasn't some elaborate dream. She was really here, trapped in a world she had only ever studied from her books and manuscripts.

She stepped out into the corridor, the cool flagstones beneath her feet sending a shiver through her. She had no plan, no idea what to do next, but staying hidden wasn't an option. She needed information, needed to blend in until she could figure out her next move.

A young woman approached, her face lighting up as she saw Eliza. "There you are! Mistress Anne has been asking for her ladies. She's in her chambers."

Eliza blinked, her mind scrambling to keep up. Mistress Anne? She knew she had to respond, to play along,but her mouth felt dry, her voice unwilling to cooperate. "I— I'm sorry, I was just—"

The girl laughed,a carefree sound that echoed in the hallway. "No need to apologise Just come quickly. You know how she hates to be kept waiting."

Without waiting for a response,she grabbed Eliza's hand,pulling her down the corridor. Eliza stumbled,struggling to keep up as they weaved through the maze of passages. The walls seemed to close in around her, the sounds of court life a maelstrom in her ears.

Her heart pounded as they rounded a corner, the ornate door at the end of the hall looming larger with each step. This was it. She was about to meet Anne Boleyn—not as a historian, not as an observer,but as someone in her service and a time traveller too.

Eliza took a deep breath, steeling herself. She would find a way through this, and she would find a way back. But for now, she had to survive in a world she had only ever read about, among people who had no idea where she had come from. But as she looked around,taking in the sights and sounds of the bustling Tudor palace,she couldn't shake the feeling that her journey was only just beginning.

Eliza knew from her history books that that Cardinal Thomas Wolsey,once the most powerful man in England next to the King,had risen to his position through his keen political acumen and service to Henry VIII. His grand residence, Hampton Court Palace,was a testament to his wealth and influence. Originally intended as a showpiece of his power, the palace was designed to rival any royal residence. But it was this very symbol of his success that would mark his downfall.

Also Wolsey's failure to secure the King,s much-desired annulment from Katherine of Aragon was his undoing. Katherine, the Spanish princess, had been married first to Henry's older brother, Arthur. Their marriage, however, was brief.
Prince Arthur died at Ludlow Castle not long after the wedding, reportedly without consummating the marriage. Katherine was left in a precarious position,a widow at a young age in a foreign land.

For years,Katherine's status hung in the balance. Her marriage to Henry was delayed, as political manoeuvring and negotiations with Spain continued. Finally, after assurances were given that the marriage with Arthur had not been consummated, Pope Julius II granted a dispensation, allowing Katherine to marry Henry. The young couple seemed hopeful, but after twenty years of marriage, only one child had survived infancy,a daughter,

Mary. The lack of a male heir was a source of growing frustration and concern for Henry, who feared the future of the Tudor dynasty.

The situation reached a breaking point when Henry became enamoured with Anne Boleyn, a young and ambitious lady of the court. Anne,with her charm and intelligence,refused to become just another of Henry's mistresses. She demanded more: she would be his wife and Queen. Henry,captivated and determined to have a legitimate male heir,sought a way to dissolve his marriage to Katherine,who was resolutely opposed to the idea. The matter of the annulment became known as the "Great Matter," consuming the court and the realm for years.

Wolsey,as Henry's chief advisor and the man responsible for obtaining the annulment, found himself in an impossible position. The Pope,under pressure from Katherine's nephew,the powerful Emperor Charles V, refused to grant the annulment. Wolsey's repeated attempts to find a solution failed,and his influence waned. Henry, impatient and desperate, blamed Wolsey for the impasse.

In a dramatic turn of events, Wolsey was stripped of his power and properties. As a gesture to appease Anne, who was becoming ever more influential,Henry seized Hampton Court from Wolsey and gifted it to her. This grand palace,with its sprawling grounds and opulent rooms,was meant to be a symbol of Anne's imminent rise to becoming the Queen.

The King,s desire to marry Anne and secure an heir led to a schism with the Catholic Church. Unable to obtain the Pope's approval,Henry took drastic measures,breaking with Rome and establishing the Church of England. This act, which fundamentally altered the religious landscape of the country,was driven as much by Henry's personal ambitions as by theological disagreements. The result was a divided nation,with the Protestant Reformation taking root in England,while many remained loyal to the old Catholic faith.

Anne Boleyn, now at the height of her influence,stood as a symbol of this new order. Her presence at Hampton Court marked the transformation of the Palace from Wolsey's seat of power to the centre of the new,reformed English court. Yet, this triumph would be short-lived. The very forces that had elevated Anne to queenship,ambition, political manoeuvring, and Henry's relentless will,would soon conspire against her,setting the stage for her dramatic and tragic fall.

Hampton Court, with its grand halls and intricate tapestries, would witness not only the splendour and celebration,s,but also the shadows of betrayal and loss that would follow. It stood as a silent testament to the capriciousness of power and the fleeting nature of favour in the turbulent world of the Tudor court and the new world that Eliza now found herself in.

Chapter Two: A Strange Arrival

The cold air of the Palace courtyard was a sharp contrast to the warmth of the study, Eliza had left behind. She shivered,feeling the material of her dress chafe against her skin. People moved around her with purpose,their chatter a murmur of incomprehensible words. Her heart pounded in her chest,a rapid drumbeat of fear and excitement. She was in Tudor England,actually here,in the midst of history.

Trying to remain inconspicuous,Eliza followed her companion to the side of the courtyard,her eyes scanning her surroundings. She had read countless books about this period,but nothing had prepared her for the reality of it: the vibrant colours of the clothing,the earthy smells,the sense of vitality that permeated everything. It was overwhelming,almost too much to process.

Eliza's heart skipped a beat. Mistress Boleyn. Could it be? She followed the woman,her mind racing. She had to think quickly,to blend in and avoid suspicion. But she also needed to get close to Anne,to see for herself the woman behind the legend.

As they entered the main hall,Eliza had to catch her breath. The room was a stunning blend of grandeur and intimacy,with rich tapestries lining the walls and a long table set with gleaming silverware. At the far end, a group of women clustered around a central figure.

Eliza recognised her from the painting she had seen and here she was.

It was Anne Boleyn in the flesh and Eliza could not believe her eyes and could have broken down in tears, from the emotion she felt.

Eliza's heart pounded as she saw her for the first time,not as a distant historical figure,but as a living,breathing woman. Anne was striking and beautiful,her dark eyes lively and intelligent,her movements graceful and assured. She wore a gown of deep emerald,the fabric shimmering in the candlelight, and her hair was swept up beneath a delicate French hood.

Eliza still felt a surge of overwhelming emotion,admiration, awe, and a strange sense of protectiveness. This was the woman who captivated a King,challenged the foundations of a kingdom,and sadly,would meet the most undeserving of ends. And Eliza was here,in her presence,with the possible opportunity to try to know her as she truly was.

"Who is this?" Anne's voice broke through,sharp and clear. She was looking directly at her,one eyebrow arched in question.

The older woman who had brought Eliza forward, cleared her throat. "A new girl, Mistress. She seemed a bit lost,but I'm sure she'll be of use."
Anne's gaze lingered on Eliza,assessing her. Eliza struggled to keep her expression neutral, though her heart was racing. She needed to say something,to make a good impression.

"I'm—Eliza Whitmore,Mistress" she said, choosing her own name instinctively. "I've come from… the North. I was hoping to find a place in your household."

For a moment,she feared she had made a mistake,but Anne's lips curved into a faint smile. "Eliza from the North.How very nice"
Anne's smile widened,a glint of curiosity in her eyes. "Well,Eliza from the North,we could use another set of hands. Times are changing, and we need those who are loyal and quick-witted."
She glanced at the older woman, who nodded in approval. "Have her join the others and ensure she's properly settled."

Eliza felt a rush of relief mixed with a nervous excitement. She had passed the first test. As the older woman led her away,she took one last look at Anne. This was just the beginning,but already she felt the weight of what lay ahead. How could she navigate this world,a world she had only known through books and lectures? And more importantly,how could she get close enough to Anne to understand her true nature,to see the real woman behind the myths?

They moved through a series of narrow hallways,the stone walls cold and rough to the touch. Servants bustled past,carrying linens and trays, their eyes lowered, their steps hurried. Eliza tried to absorb every detail,the clipped accents,the way the women moved,the scents of herbs and wax that permeated the air. Everything felt foreign,yet familiar,like stepping into the pages of a Tudor history book she had read countless times.
The woman finally stopped in a small chamber, sparsely furnished with wooden stools and a table strewn with sewing materials. "This is where you'll start," she said briskly. "You're to help with the sewing and mending until you're needed elsewhere. If you've any sense,you'll keep your head down and your mouth shut. Mistress Boleyn has no patience for idle gossip."
Eliza nodded, murmuring her thanks. The woman's stern expression softened slightly."You're a long way from home, lass. Keep your wits about you,and you'll be fine." With that,she turned and left,the door closing behind her with a solid thud.

Eliza stood alone for a moment,taking it all in. She was actually here,in Anne Boleyn's household,a witness to history in the making. The enormity of it threatened to overwhelm her,but she forced herself to focus. She had to keep her cover,to learn as much as she could without drawing attention.

A small group of women entered the room, their eyes curious as they took in the new arrival. Eliza smiled, trying to appear calm and friendly. "I'm Eliza," she said."I'm new here."

One of the women,a fair-haired girl with a warm smile,stepped forward. "I'm Mary. Welcome to the madness." There was a hint of humour in her voice, and Eliza felt a flicker of gratitude. "Don't worry,we don't bite. Just keep up with the sewing,and you'll be fine."

The others nodded in agreement,their smiles genuine,but guarded.

Eliza took a seat and began to work,her fingers clumsy with the unfamiliar needle and thread. The women chatted quietly as they stitched,their talk centred on the daily routines and gossip of the court. Eliza listened carefully,absorbing every word.

It soon became clear that the atmosphere in Anne's household was tense. Whispers of political manoeuvring of alliances and betrayals, filled the air. Anne was close to the King,but there were those who resented her rise,who saw her as a threat to the established order.

The women spoke of courtiers who would smile to her face and plot against her behind closed doors.

As the hours passed,Eliza's mind raced. She had known the broad strokes of Anne's story,but hearing it first hand was something else entirely. Anne wasn't just a figurehead or a pawn—she was a woman of ambition, intelligence, and courage,navigating a world that was both glamorous and perilous. And Eliza was now a part of that world,her world,however small her role might be.

By the time the day ended, Eliza's hands were sore and her back ached. She had managed to avoid too many questions,but she knew it wouldn't be long before her new companions grew curious. She needed a plan,a way to gain Anne's trust and learn more about her true character.

But first, she needed rest.

That night,Eliza lay on a narrow cot in a small,shared chamber, her thoughts a whirlwind of fear and excitement.

She was in Tudor England,actually working for Anne Boleyn,witnessing history unfold before her eyes.

Absolutely incredible,but what would happen next?

How could she change anything,if at all?

And what if she was trapped here,unable to return to her own time?

As sleep finally overtook her,Eliza resolved to take things one step at a time. She would watch, listen, and learn.

And she would find a way to understand the real Anne Boleyn,the woman who had captivated the most powerful man in England and changed the course of history forever with the Reformation.

Chapter Three: Into the Court's Web

The morning sun streamed through the narrow windows of the chamber, casting a soft,golden light over the room. Eliza awoke to the sounds of the Palace coming to life,voices calling, doors creaking,and the rhythmic clatter of hooves in the courtyard below. She sat up,her body still heavy with sleep,and took a moment to remember where she was.

The surreal events of the previous day flooded back,and she felt a jolt of anxiety mixed with exhilaration.

After washing herself in a bowl of cold water,putting on the simple blue gown left for her and finding a hair clip of some sort,pinned her hair up and put it under a coif,then Eliza made her way to the hall where the women of Anne's household gathered each morning. They were already busy,some carrying trays of food,others whispering as they arranged flowers and linens. The air buzzed with anticipation. Today,Anne was to meet with important visitors,and the household was abuzz with preparations. Mary,the young woman who had been kind to her the day before,caught Eliza's eye and waved her over."Eliza,you're to help with the flowers today. Mistress Boleyn wants everything to be perfect."

Eliza nodded, feeling a mix of relief and nervousness. This would be her first real test, working in close proximity to Anne. She followed Mary to a corner where several women were arranging bouquets of roses and lavender. The scent was intoxicating, filling the air with a sweet, heady fragrance.

As they worked, Mary chatted softly. "It's quite the honour to be part of Mistress Boleyn's household, you know. She's close to the King,and her star is rising. But it's not an easy life. There are many who would see her fall."

Eliza glanced at her,sensing a deeper meaning beneath the casual tone. "Do you think she'll succeed?" she asked carefully.

Mary shrugged,her eyes thoughtful. "She's clever, and she has the King,s favour,and this court... it's like a spider's web. One wrong step, and you're caught. You would be best to remember that,Eliza ."

Eliza nodded,her stomach tightening. She was beginning to understand the danger of the game that Anne was playing. The Tudor court was a place of shifting alliances and hidden threats,where even a whisper could lead to ruin.

Their conversation was interrupted by a flurry of activity at the far end of the hall. Anne had entered,surrounded by her ladies-in-waiting.

She was dressed in a gown of rich crimson,her dark hair falling in loose waves over her shoulders. Her presence was magnetic,commanding the attention of everyone in the room.

Eliza watched as Anne moved through the hall,speaking briefly to each of her attendants,her voice low and confident. When she reached the corner where Eliza and Mary were working,she paused,her gaze sweeping over the floral arrangements.

"These are lovely," Anne said,her eyes lingering on the bouquets.

"Make sure they're placed in the main chamber. I want everything to be perfect for our guests."

Mary curtsied,her face lighting up with a pleased smile.

"Yes, Mistress. We'll see to it."

Anne's gaze shifted to Eliza,her expression curious.

"Eliza,Yes? I trust you're settling in well?"

Eliza,s heart raced. "Yes, Mistress.Thank you."

Anne nodded, her lips curving into a slight smile.

"Good.There's much to be done,and I need people I can rely on."

With that, she moved on,her presence like a passing storm,leaving a trail of admiration and unease in her wake. Eliza let out a breath she hadn't realised she was holding. It had been a brief encounter,but it had left her shaken. There was a strength in Anne,a sense of purpose and resolve that was both inspiring and intimidating.

As the day progressed,the household buzzed with activity. Eliza found herself drawn into the whirlwind of preparations,her thoughts a constant swirl of curiosity and caution. She observed everything,the way the servants moved,the snippets of conversation she overheard,the subtle glances exchanged among the courtiers.

By midday,the Palace was ready to receive its visitors. Eliza, along with the other attendants,was stationed discreetly around the main hall, ready to assist as needed. She watched as a procession of noble gentlemen and ladies arrived,their clothes rich and ornate,their expressions a careful mask of politeness and intrigue.

When King Henry VIII himself entered the room,Eliza felt a jolt of shock. She had read so much about him,his larger-than-life personality and commanding presence,his charisma and ruthlessness,but seeing him in person was something else entirely.

He was a magnificent towering figure clothed in a gold and crimson velvet doublet and hose and white stockings and slip on shoes to match and positioned on his head, a black velvet cap with a feather gently swaying,showcasing,his copper coloured hair beneath. His presence filled the space,his eyes sharp and calculating as he surveyed the room.

This was the man that Eliza had studied many times,who was the most handsome Prince in Christendom when he became King in 1509,on the death of his father,King Henry V11.

Eliza was awestruck at seeing the actual Henry in person. He was a fine figure of a man.

Anne moved to greet him,her face lit with a smile that seemed both genuine and strategic. The King's gaze softened as he looked at her,his expression almost tender. Eliza watched,fascinated,as they spoke quietly, their voices too low to catch.

Chapter Four: The First Mission

Eliza had now been in this strange,but interesting Tudor world for a few weeks now and was being seen as someone trustworthy and so the air outside Greenwich Palace was crisp and cool,that morning as Eliza stepped into the bustling streets of London. The city was a cacophony of sounds,hawkers shouting their wares,horses clattering on cobblestones,the distant tolling of church bells. The scent of smoke and spices mixed with the earthy tang of the Thames,a sharp contrast to the more refined fragrances within Anne's household.

Eliza pulled her cloak tightly around her shoulders,the weight of Anne's letter hidden beneath it like a secret burning against her skin.

She had only a vague idea of where Cheapside was located and an even hazier plan of what she would do once she got there. But she had no choice; she had to trust her instincts and hope she could find the right house without drawing unwanted attention.

Navigating the streets was both exhilarating and disorienting. It was one thing to read about Tudor London,to see its layout in books and maps, but it was another to walk its crooked lanes and narrow alleyways. The city felt alive,pulsing with energy and danger. Eliza kept her head down, blending in with the throngs of people,her eyes scanning the street signs and shopfronts for any indication that she was heading in the right direction.

Cheapside, when she finally reached it,was a bustling thoroughfare, lined with shops and stalls selling everything from fine cloth to exotic spices. Merchants called out to passersby,their voices a constant din, while apprentices darted through the crowd carrying bundles and baskets. Eliza moved carefully,conscious of the letter in her possession. The instructions had been vague—just a house,unremarkable, a man who would know what to do. But how would she find it among so many?

She slowed her pace, scanning the buildings,looking for some clue. The houses were close-packed,their upper stories jutting out over the street, casting long shadows in the sun. She noticed a small,nondescript building set back slightly from the others,its door plain and unadorned. Something about it seemed right,though she couldn't have said why.

Eliza took a deep breath and approached the door.

She knocked softly,her heart pounding in her ears. For a moment,there was no response. She was about to knock again when the door creaked open a sliver,revealing a narrow slice of shadowed interior. A man's face appeared,lined and wary,his eyes sharp as he looked her over.

"Yes?"His voice was low,almost a growl. "What do you want?"

Eliza swallowed,forcing herself to stay calm. "I've come from Mistress Anne Boleyn," she said quietly. "She has sent me with a message."

The man's eyes narrowed,and he glanced quickly up and down the street before opening the door wider. "Come in, quickly."

Eliza slipped inside,the door closing behind her with a soft thud. The interior was dimly lit,the air heavy with the scent of smoke and ink. Shelves lined the walls,filled with books and papers,and a small fire crackled in the hearth. The man motioned for her to sit at a rough wooden table in the centre of the room.

"Show me," he said, his voice still guarded.

Eliza reached into her bodice and pulled out the letter,her hands trembling slightly. She placed it on the table,and the man picked it up, examining the seal closely before breaking it open. He read the letter quickly,his eyes flicking over the words,his expression unreadable.

When he finished,he looked up at her,his gaze thoughtful. "You're new, aren't you? I haven't seen you before."

Eliza nodded,unsure of how much to say."Yes,I have only recently joined Mistress Anne's household."

The man grunted,folding the letter carefully and tucking it into his tunic.

"Well, you've done well to bring this to me. There are many who would love to get their hands on her correspondence."

Eliza's pulse quickened."Is she in danger?"

The man's expression softened slightly,and he gave a small, grim smile. "In danger? Mistress Boleyn lives in a world of danger. Every word she speaks,every move she makes is watched and judged. There are those who would see her brought down, and they would use any means necessary."

He paused,studying her. "But you're not just worried for her, are you? You're worried for yourself."

Eliza hesitated, then nodded. "I… I don't know who to trust. This world… it's not what I'm used to."

The man leaned back,his gaze steady. "If you're loyal to Mistress Boleyn, you need to be careful. There are spies everywhere,even among those who seem friendly. And if you find yourself in trouble,you mustn't hesitate to seek help."

Eliza,s mind raced. Who was this man? Why was he so protective of Anne? But she knew better than to ask too many questions.

"Thank you," she said quietly. "I'll remember that."

The man nodded, standing up. "You should go now. It's not safe for you to be seen here too long. I'll make sure this letter reaches its destination."

Eliza rose,her legs feeling unsteady beneath her.

"Thank you. Please,tell Mistress Boleyn I delivered it safely."

"I will," he said, opening the door for her. "And be careful, Eliza,the court is a dangerous place,especially for those who walk close to the flame."

Eliza stepped back into the bustling street,her mind swirling.The man's words had left her more unsettled than before. Anne was in more danger than she had realised,and Eliza was now entangled in whatever plots and schemes were brewing around her.

As she made her way back,she tried to piece together what little she knew. Who was the man she had just met? An ally of Anne's,clearly,but why such secrecy? And what was in the letter that was so important?

Eliza would find out a few days later that the man to whom she gave the letter from Anne,was Thomas Wyatt. Thomas Wyatt is a poet and diplomat,and he has a complex relationship with Anne. Eliza does not know their exact connection as it is not known,but she was told that it is believed they are close friends and possibly more,before Anne's involvement with Henry VIII. Wyatt serves as a trusted intermediary,discreetly passing Anne's messages and maintaining her network of communication within the court. His role is crucial,as he helps Anne navigate the treacherous political landscape while also serving as a confidant and ally.

When she finally returned to Anne's household,the sun was beginning to set, casting long shadows across the courtyard.Eliza slipped back inside,her steps silent on the flagstones.She needed to find a way to learn more,to understand the full scope of what was happening around her. But for now,she would have to be patient.
Eliza entered the hall where the other servants were bustling about, preparing for the evening. Mary caught sight of her and hurried over,her face alight with curiosity. "Well? Did you deliver the message?" Mary asked,her voice low.
Eliza nodded, forcing a smile. "Yes,everything went smoothly."
Mary looked relieved. "Good. Mistress Boleyn will be pleased. You're fitting in well,Eliza. Just remember to keep your head down and don't get involved in anything too complicated."
Eliza smiled,though her thoughts were far from simple. She was already involved,more deeply than Mary could imagine.
And she knew that this was only the beginning.
As the evening wore on and the household settled into its routine,Eliza found herself thinking of Anne,of the strength and resolve she had seen in her eyes,of the risks she was taking in her quest for power and recognition. It was easy to see why history had painted her as ambitious, even ruthless. But Eliza sensed there was

more to Anne's story,a complexity that went beyond the usual tales of seduction and betrayal.

And Eliza was determined to uncover it,to understand the real woman behind the legend.

For now,she would continue to play her part,to observe and learn. But she would also be cautious,for the court was a place of shadows and secrets,and one misstep could be her undoing.

She would find a way to get closer to Anne,to see the truth of her life and her choices. And she would do it without losing herself in the process.

Chapter Five: Unveiling Secrets

The dim light of dawn crept into Greenwich Palace as Eliza awoke,her body still weary from the previous day's journey to Cheapside. She stretched,wincing at the stiffness in her muscles. Today would be another challenging day,navigating court politics, balancing her role as a servant,and staying close to Anne without drawing too much attention.

After dressing in the plain red gown she'd been provided with,Eliza made her way to the servants' quarters,where the morning bustle was already in full swing. Trays of bread and jugs of ale were being prepared for breakfast,and the air was filled with the smell of baking. She greeted Mary with a nod as she took up her duties,focusing on the mundane tasks that grounded her in this strange,new world.

But her mind kept drifting back to Cheapside and the letter she had delivered. What secrets did it contain? And what kind of danger was Anne truly in? She had come to the Tudor court seeking answers,but every step deeper seemed to only raise more questions.

As the morning wore on,Eliza noticed Anne moving through the hall,her presence commanding attention. Courtiers and servants alike glanced her way with varying degrees of awe and apprehension. Even though Anne was not yet Queen,her influence was undeniable.
Today, she seemed particularly vibrant,a quiet confidence radiating from her.
Eliza seized the opportunity. She needed to find a way to gain Anne's trust,to learn more about her inner circle and the enemies who sought to destroy her. As Anne approached, Eliza stepped forward,carefully balancing a tray of breakfast items.

"Good morning, Mistress," she said softly, bowing her head in deference.
Anne paused,her eyes alight with recognition.
"Ah,Eliza.You were successful yesterday?"
"Yes, Mistress," Eliza replied, keeping her voice low. "It was delivered as you instructed."
Anne's gaze lingered on her, thoughtful. "I appreciate your discretion, Eliza. It is not always easy to know whom to trust."
Eliza hesitated, then took a risk. "If I may, Mistress,I wish to be of greater service to you. I know that I am new here,but I am loyal. And I believe I could help in more ways than just delivering letters."
Anne's eyes narrowed slightly, as if weighing the sincerity of Eleanor's words. "You are bold, Eliza. And boldness can be a dangerous trait at court."

Eliza dipped her head, her heart racing. "I understand, Mistress. I only wish to serve you as best I can."

There was a long pause, during which Eliza felt her pulse thundering in her ears. Then Anne smiled, a faint but genuine expression. "Very well. I will keep your offer in mind. For now, continue with your duties. But know that I will call on you if I have need."

Relief and excitement mingled in Eliza,s chest. "Thank you, Mistress. I will not let you down."

Anne nodded, a flicker of something unreadable in her eyes.

"See that you do not."

With that, she turned and continued down the hall, leaving Eliza standing there, her heart still pounding. It wasn't much, but it was a start. Anne had noticed her, acknowledged her. And that was more than Eliza could have hoped for, so soon.

Over the next few days, Eliza threw herself into her work, careful to remain diligent and unassuming. But she kept a watchful eye on Anne and those who interacted with her. She noticed the subtle alliances and rivalries among the courtiers, the way whispers and glances spoke volumes more than words.

It was during one such observation that Eliza caught sight of a figure she recognized from her historical studies, Thomas Cromwell, the king's chief minister. He was a formidable presence, his expression stern and calculating as he moved through the court. Eliza felt a shiver run down her spine. Cromwell was known for his ruthlessness, his ability to rise and fall those around him with a mere word. If he was involved in whatever plots were swirling around Anne,things could become dangerous very quickly.

One afternoon,as Eliza was attending to her tasks,she overheard a conversation between two of Anne's ladies-in-waiting. They were speaking in hushed tones,their faces tense.

As they moved to the corner of the room,one said" Cromwell has been meeting with the king more frequently," one of them whispered."There are rumours he is advising against Mistress Boleyn's marriage with the King."

The other lady glanced around nervously. "But why? What does he gain by opposing her? The King's affections are clear."

"Yes,but Cromwell has his own agenda. They say he seeks to strengthen ties with Spain,and Mistress Boleyn is an obstacle to that."

Eliza's heart sank. Cromwell was a master manipulator,and if he was turning the King's favour against Anne,then the stakes were higher than she had realised. Anne's position was precarious, and Eliza knew that any misstep could lead to disaster.

That evening,Eliza found herself alone in the gardens,her mind churning with everything she had learned. The soft murmur of a fountain nearby was the only sound as she paced,trying to piece together the fragments of information she had gathered. Anne was ambitious,yes,but she was also vulnerable. And Eliza felt a growing sense of responsibility,not just to observe history,but to protect the woman she was coming to admire.

A soft rustle behind her made Eliza turn.

Anne stood there,watching her with a curious expression.The royal gardens at dusk with the scent of roses filled the air,and a soft breeze rustled the leaves of the hedges. Anne strolled along the path,her hands lightly grazing the flowers. Eliza approached her,her mind still reeling, from her meeting with Thomas Cromwell.

 "There you are. I've been looking for you. You seem troubled.
Is something weighing on your mind?"
Eliza,pausing for a moment,taking in Anne's serene, yet regal presence "I had a meeting with Master Cromwell… He is not a man who offers peace easily."
Anne,narrowed her eyes "Cromwell… always scheming. He serves the King,but his ambitions serve himself. You must be careful around him. He knows more than he lets on,and he uses every secret to his advantage."
Eliza,nodded,her thoughts drifting to her own secret "Yes, he is always watching. Looking for weaknesses in others to strengthen his own position. He asked me many questions, too many, as if searching for something hidden."
Anne frowning, stepped closer "What did he ask you, Eliza?"
Eliza spoke carefully "He asked about my past,where I came from. It was… unsettling."
Anne,her voice laced with concern."And what did you tell him?"
Eliza,her heart quickening "Only what I could. I told him enough to satisfy his curiosity,but not everything. Some truths are better left unsaid."
Anne,sensing something deeper "You speak in riddles sometimes, Eliza. There's something about you… as if

you carry the weight of many lifetimes. Tell me, what is it that you are hiding?"

Eliza,her gaze shifting to the horizon, the soft glow of the setting sun casting shadows across the garden, "If I could tell you,Mistress, I would. But there are things… things you wouldn't believe even if I told you."

Anne,reaching out, gently touching Eliza's arm "Try me."

Eliza,her voice faltering "There are moments when I feel I don't belong here. As though I've stepped out of time,watching events unfold that I… already know."
She took a deep breath,choosing her words carefully.
"Do you ever feel as though you are being pulled by something larger than yourself,as if you are walking a path that was set long before you even knew it existed?"
Anne,nodded slowly,her gaze thoughtful "I feel that every day. My rise to the throne,my love for the King,the weight of England upon my shoulders… It is as if I am playing a role in a story that was written long ago. But you… you speak of it as if you've seen it."

Eliza,her voice soft, almost a whisper "I have seen things,Mistress. Things that have not yet come to pass. I know the dangers that lie ahead,the schemes of men like Cromwell. I know how fragile this moment is for you… for all of us."

Anne,her eyes widening slightly "What are you saying, Eliza? How could you know such things?"

Eliza,her heart pounding as she walked the fine line between truth and secrecy "I've spent years studying the ways of power,how empires rise and fall,how men like Cromwell twist the world to their advantage. But there is more to it than that. There are times when I feel as though

I'm living these moments for the second time,watching history unfold before my eyes."

Anne,her voice barely above a whisper "You speak as though you have lived this before."

Eliza,hesitating,then looking directly into Anne's eyes "In a way, I have. The things I've read,the things I've seen… they are like echoes of a world that has already been. I came to you because I believe you are at the centre of something great, Mistress. But greatness comes with danger, and those like Cromwell… they won't rest until they find a way to take you down."

Anne,her voice quiet, but full of resolve "And what of the future you speak of? What is to become of me?"

Eliza was feeling the weight of her knowledge,her heart was feeling very heavy "The future's not set in stone. But there are… shadows that loom ahead. That is why I cannot tell you everything,Mistress. There are things I wish I could change, things I would warn you of… but some events,no matter how much we wish to alter them,cannot be undone."

Anne,her voice now full of suspicion and curiosity "You speak of destiny as though you've seen it. But you won't tell me what you know."

Eliza,stepping closer, lowering her voice "It is not that I won't tell you, it's that I can't. Some things,must happen as they are meant to. But I can promise you this,Mistress,I will do everything in my power to protect you from those who seek to harm you."

Anne,her eyes searching Eliza's face,her voice softening "You are a strange comfort to me,Eliza. There is something about you that feels… otherworldly. And yet,I trust you more than I trust most."

Eliza,smiled faintly,her heart aching with the burden of what she cannot say "And I will stand by you,Mistress. Through whatever storms come our way."

Anne was gazing at the garden, her mind turning over Eliza's cryptic words "Cromwell may plot, and others may scheme,but I will not falter. Not yet."

Eliza spoke quietly,to herself "Not yet..."

Chapter Six: Shadows in the Court

The air in the court was thick with tension. Whispers filled the corridors, carrying rumours and speculation that only heightened Eliza,s anxiety. As she moved through the Palace,her mind raced with thoughts of Cromwell and his machinations. Every glance,every fleeting conversation seemed to hold a hidden meaning,a thread that could unravel everything Anne had worked for.

Anne,however,remained outwardly composed. She maintained her poised demeanour,engaging with courtiers and nobles with the same grace and intelligence that had drawn Henry's attention in the first place. But Eliza,who had begun to understand the nuances of Anne's expressions,could see the strain behind her smiles.

A few days after their conversation in the gardens,Anne summoned Eliza to her private chambers. As Eliza entered ,she noticed a large map spread across the table, along with several letters written in a neat, precise hand.

"Come in, Eliza," Anne said,her voice calm but her eyes intense. "There is much to discuss."

Eliza stepped forward, her curiosity piqued.

"What would you have me do, Mistress?"

Anne gestured to the map and the letters. "I need you to help me gather information. My future,and that of England,depends on securing alliances. Cromwell is undermining me at every turn, and I must know who is loyal and who is not."

Eliza,s heart pounded. This was more than she had anticipated. She had hoped to assist Anne,to be her confidante and support,but now she was being drawn into the very heart of Tudor politics.

"I will do my best,Mistress," she said, her voice steady despite the nerves she felt. "What do you need me to find out?"

Anne smiled faintly. "There are certain courtiers and ambassadors I am unsure of. I need to know where their true loyalties lie. Who they speak with,what their intentions are. It is delicate work,Eliza,and dangerous."

"I understand," Eliza replied. She glanced at the letters,recognizing some of the names,nobles and diplomats she had read about in her studies,their fates intertwined with Anne's rise and fall.

Anne stepped closer,her gaze piercing. "You must be discreet. Trust no one. Even those who appear friendly may have their own agendas."

Eliza nodded. "I will be careful."

For the next few weeks, Eliza,s life took on a new rhythm. She continued her duties as a servant,but her eyes and ears were always open,searching for clues,piecing together the intricate web of alliances and betrayals that defined Henry's court. She found herself shadowing certain courtiers,lingering near conversations,noting who spoke with whom and what was said.

It was exhausting work,and the constant vigilance took its toll. But Eliza knew how crucial it was. Each evening,she would report back to Anne, sharing what she had learned. Some information was trivial,but other pieces painted a clearer picture of the forces arrayed against her.

One evening,as Eliza recounted a particularly tense conversation between two noblemen,Anne's expression darkened after Eliza described them to Anne.

"So,it is as I feared," Anne murmured. "My Lord Norfolk is moving against me."

Eliza,s stomach tightened. "He spoke with Cromwell. I couldn't hear everything,but it was clear they are conspiring."

Anne's hands clenched at her sides. "Norfolk is my uncle,but he would see me fall if it served his interests. I had hoped he would support me, but he is a snake, like so many others here."

Eliza hesitated,then spoke carefully. "What will you do, Mistress?"

Anne's eyes flashed with determination. "I will do what I must. I will fight. But I need more information. We must find out exactly what Cromwell is planning,and how deep his influence runs."

Over the following days,Eliza,s role grew even more complex. She began to interact more directly with the courtiers,using her position as a seemingly inconspicuous servant to strike up conversations and gather intelligence. She was careful,always careful,to avoid arousing suspicion. But it was a dangerous game.

One afternoon,while delivering a message to the queen's apartments, Eliza found herself cornered by Thomas Cromwell again. His presence was formidable, his dark eyes cold and unreadable as he faced her.

"You are Mistress Boleyn's servant,are you not?" he asked,his tone casual,but his gaze sharp.

"Yes,My Lord," Eliza replied,keeping her head bowed. Her heart pounded so loudly she was sure he could hear it.

Cromwell tilted his head slightly, as if considering her. "She has been... very active of late. I wonder if you might have noticed anything unusual."

Eliza swallowed,choosing her words carefully. "Mistress Boleyn is dedicated to her duties, my Lord. She is focused on serving the King."

Cromwell's lips curved into a thin smile. "Of course she is. But you see, it is my duty to ensure that all is well within the court. To root out any... disturbances. I would hate to think that anyone close to Mistress Boleyn might be causing trouble."

Eliza forced herself to remain calm. "I only wish to serve my mistress faithfully, my Lord."

Cromwell's smile did not reach his eyes. "I am sure you do. But remember,loyalty can be a dangerous thing if misplaced."

With that,he turned and walked away,leaving Eliza shaken,but resolved. Cromwell was onto her,or at least suspicious. She would have to be more cautious than ever.

That night,as she recounted the encounter to Anne,the tension between them was palpable.

"He knows," Anne whispered,her voice tight with fear and anger. "That horrible man knows I am gathering information. We must be more careful."

Eliza nodded,her mind racing. "What should we do, Mistress?"

Anne's expression hardened. "We press on. We cannot let him see that he has shaken us. But we must be vigilant."

Back in her chambers and alone with Eliza,Anne sighed, rubbing her temples"These days feel endless. The court, the whispers, the pressure,it's overwhelming. I don't know how much longer I can handle it."
Eliza watched her with concern "You carry so much, Mistress. But... what if I told you that the future holds things you can't even imagine?"
Anne frowning, intrigued "The future? What do you mean by that?"
Eliza,choosing her words carefully "There are ways of knowing things, things that seem impossible. Sometimes, I feel like I can see glimpses,of what might happen, what could be." She pauses. "You are not just a fleeting figure in this world. Your legacy,your daughter,will change England forever."
Anne, her brow furrowing "My daughter? But I haven't had a son yet. How can a daughter...?"
Eliza softly "Sometimes,greatness doesn't come in the way people expect. Sometimes,it's the ones people overlook who change the course of history. Elizabeth..." She hesitates. "Your child will be extraordinary."

Anne growing more intrigued, but also cautious"How do you know this, Eliza? What kind of talk is this,do you have some gift of prophecy,or is this just a fantasy?"
Eliza with a small,comforting smile "Let's just say I've seen things that others haven't. I see you,Mistress,not just as you are now,but as history will remember you. You

will be remembered long after the struggles you face here."

Anne her eyes narrowing "Remembered? You speak as though I should prepare for some great struggle."

Eliza gently "In a way, you are already in the middle of one. But you aren't alone,and what's to come isn't as dark as it may seem. You have an important role to play. The world will remember you,not just for now, but for what you leave behind."

Anne leaned forward, intrigued but suspicious"You're speaking in riddles,Eliza. But there's something in your words that stirs something in me. What are you not telling me?"

Eliza, with a sad smile"I wish I could tell you everything. But some things are better left unsaid. For now,trust me when I say... There are better days ahead. What you're going through,what you're sacrificing,it will mean something."

Anne relaxing a little,still intrigued, but not pushing further "You are a strange one,Eliza. But there's something in your eyes... something I can't place. Very well, I'll trust you. But do not make me regret it."

Eliza then said softly "I will do everything I can to help you. I promise."

As Eliza left Anne's chambers that night, she felt the weight of her role pressing down on her. She had come to Tudor England seeking to understand Anne Boleyn,but now she was part of a struggle that could determine the course of history itself and she wanted so much to tell her more.

In the days that followed,Eliza's senses were on high alert. Every conversation,every glance,every whisper seemed fraught with danger. She continued to gather what information she could,reporting back to Anne whenever she had something of value. But the atmosphere at court was growing more oppressive,the tension so thick it felt like it could snap at any moment.

One evening,as Eliza made her way back to her quarters,she noticed a shadowy figure following her. She quickened her pace,her heart racing. She turned a corner,then another,trying to lose her pursuer. But the figure was relentless,always a few steps behind. Finally,she ducked into a small alcove, pressing herself against the wall. She held her breath,listening as the footsteps drew closer. Then they stopped. Eliza,s pulse thundered in her ears as she waited,every muscle tense. After what felt like an eternity, the footsteps retreated. Eliza exhaled shakily,her body trembling with adrenaline. She had narrowly escaped, but it was a stark reminder of how precarious her position was.
As she made her way back to her room,Eliza,s mind raced with thoughts of what lay ahead. Cromwell was closing in,and the court was becoming more dangerous by the day. But she couldn't turn back now. Anne needed her, and she was determined to see this through,no matter the cost.
She only hoped that she could stay one step ahead of the shadows closing in around them both.

Chapter Seven: The Queen's Gambit

The court was abuzz with speculation as Henry's plans for Anne's Coronation began to take shape. Whispers of Anne's imminent rise to being crowned Queen spread like wildfire,igniting both excitement and resentment among the courtiers. For some,Anne was the embodiment of ambition and grace,a beacon of change; for others,she was a usurper,a threat to the established order.

Eliza watched it all unfold from the fringes,her heart heavy with worry. Though Anne seemed to flourish under the attention,Eliza knew that the Coronation would mark the point of no return. Once crowned queen, Anne would be even more exposed to the machinations of those who sought her downfall.

Anne was in her chambers,in the early evening. The soft glow of candlelight filled the room. Anne stood before a large mirror, dressed in an opulent gown of gold and deep crimson,embroidered with pearls. Eliza had carefully arranged her hair,her fingers deftly weaving Anne's dark locks beneath an exquisite French hood.Just the two of them

Anne sat gazing at her reflection "Soon, Eliza,I will be crowned Queen of England."

She exhaled deeply,her eyes revealing a mix of pride and worry.

"How can one hold such power and still feel so small?"

Eliza,gently adjusting a strand of Anne's hair.

"Power isn't just in crowns or titles, Mistress. It's in how people

remember you,the legacy you leave behind. It's in what you fight for and what you protect."

Anne stood glancing at Eliza in the mirror,intrigued "You speak as though you know what will come of all this. As if you can see the future."

Eliza paused for a moment, her hands still "Those who shape history. I've always believed that certain souls are meant for more,even if the road ahead is uncertain."
Anne,her expression softening"I feel that, too. The weight of destiny,like something pulling me toward it, whether I am ready or not. But you…"
Anne turned slightly to look at Eliza.
"You speak with a calmness I envy. As though you're sure of what lies beyond this moment. Do you ever fear what the future holds?"
Eliza quietly spoke "The future is always changing. Sometimes it's a blessing not to know what comes next. But there are moments,like now, when we stand at a crossroads,and the choices we make ripple through time."
Anne frowning,curious"And what of my choice? This path I'm on,it's full of risks. I know that. The King's favour is a dangerous thing. But I can't turn back now, can I?"
Eliza met Anne's gaze in the mirror,her voice soft but firm "No, you can't turn back. You're meant to walk this path,even if you can't see where it leads. What you've begun,will echo through history."
Anne laughed lightly,though there's tension in her voice "Echoes through history. You speak as if I am already a story being told."

Eliza looked at Anne smiling, "One day,Mistress, they will tell your story. People will remember your strength,your ambition. But they will also remember the woman behind the crown. The mother,the reformer,the one who stood beside a King and changed the course of a kingdom."
Anne faced Eliza,her eyes searching "How is it that you,of all my ladies, seem to know me so well? It's as though you see more than what's in front of you."

Eliza,her heart pounding, careful with her words " I have read stories of those who rise and change the world around them. Perhaps it gives me a different perspective to know that."

Anne,smiling faintly, though still watching her): "You're different, Eliza. There's something in the way you speak,as if you've lived through these moments before."

Eliza,her voice catching slightly "In a way, I have. Watching history unfold is,like reliving it. Every moment feels familiar,and yet it's new all over again."

Anne,nodding,her expression thoughtful "I suppose this banquet, this Coronation,will be just the beginning of what's to come. But I feel as though I'm walking into a storm, and I cannot see the end of it."

Eliza,stepping forward, placed a hand gently on Anne's arm "You are stronger than the storm,Mistress. Whatever comes,you'll face it with the same courage that brought you here. You won't be forgotten,not by history,not by those who truly see you."

Anne,her eyes softening,the tension easing slightly "You speak as if you've already seen my triumphs and my trials, Eliza."

Eliza looked at Anne,smiling sadly "Perhaps I've just read more stories than most. But... whatever happens, remember that you are not alone in this. I will stand by you, as will those who believe in you."

Anne nodded, her gaze growing distant as she prepared herself for the evening ahead "It is a strange comfort,knowing you are here with me. I trust you, Eliza. More than most."

Eliza spoke quietly, as she stepped back "And I will not let you down, Mistress. Not now,not ever."

"Mistress, I will tell you this,I fear that your enemies will only grow bolder as your Coronation approaches,"she said quietly,her eyes meeting Anne's in the mirror.

Anne's gaze remained steady,her expression serene. "I am aware of the risks, Eliza. But I have worked too hard to turn back now. This is my destiny. I will be Queen, and no one,not Cromwell, not Norfolk,not even the King,s former allies,will stand in my way."

Eliza admired Anne's determination,but she couldn't shake the sense of foreboding that had settled in her chest. "Just… be cautious, Mistress. Trust no one."

Anne turned to face her,a small smile playing on her lips. "Including you?"

Eliza hesitated,then shook her head. "I am loyal to you,Mistress. I swear it."

"I know you are," Anne said softly. "And I am grateful for your friendship, Eliza. But do not worry. I have a plan."

Eliza,s curiosity was piqued. "A plan?"

Anne nodded, her eyes gleaming with a hint of mischief. "Yes. There are those who believe they can control me,manipulate me. But they underestimate my resolve. I have allies of my own,and I intend to use them."

Before Eliza could ask for more details,a tiny tap and the doors to Anne's chambers opened, and George Boleyn,Anne's brother,entered. His presence was commanding,his demeanour calm and confident.

Eliza had always felt a strange tension around George,a mixture of admiration and unease. He was fiercely loyal to Anne,but there was a ruthlessness in him that she found unsettling.

"Sister," George greeted,his voice warm. "The banquet is about to begin. The King awaits you.How are you feeling.Is the child well"

Anne smiled and rose gracefully. "Thank you, George.All is well and I will be there shortly."

As George turned to leave,he cast a quick, assessing glance at Eliza. She met his gaze steadily,refusing to be intimidated.

Once he was gone,Anne turned back to Eliza. "George is one of my most trusted allies," she said quietly. "But even he does not know everything. There are some things I must keep to myself and yes,Eliza,I am with child "

Eliza remembered her books at home had told her of Anne Boleyn being pregnant when she was crowned Queen of England in 1533,and here she was witnessing it all in person,but quickly she composed herself in the present moment,understanding the need for secrecy.

"That is wonderful news about the baby and,of course,I understand the importance of secrecy,Mistress."

Anne took a deep breath,then squared her shoulders. "Come,let us go. Tonight, we celebrate. Tomorrow,we will prepare."

The banquet was a dazzling affair, a display of opulence and power designed to remind everyone of Anne's growing influence. The hall was filled with the scent of roasted meats and spiced wine,the sound of laughter and music reverberating off the high ceilings. Eliza moved through the crowd,her senses alert,taking in the subtle shifts in mood and conversation.

She noticed Cromwell,standing near a group of nobles,his gaze fixed on Anne as she moved gracefully through the throng. His expression was inscrutable,but Eliza felt a chill run down her spine. Whatever he was planning,he was playing a long game,biding his time,but it couldn't happen yet and he knew it.

As the night wore on, Eliza managed to catch snippets of

conversations,some supportive,others laced with resentment. The divisions at court were deepening,and Anne's ascension to the throne would only widen the cracks.

During a lull in the festivities,Eliza slipped outside for some fresh air. The gardens were quiet,the cool night air a welcome respite from the heat and noise of the banquet hall. She wandered along a little path, her thoughts a whirlwind of uncertainty.

She was so lost in thought that she didn't hear the footsteps approaching until it was too late. A hand clamped over her mouth, and she was yanked backward,her back pressed against a solid,unyielding chest.

"Do not scream," a low voice hissed in her ear. "I mean you no harm."

Eliza heart pounded wildly as she struggled to break free. But the grip was firm,the voice insistent.

"Listen to me," the voice continued, a note of urgency in its tone. "I am a friend. I need to warn you."

Eliza stilled,her breath coming in ragged gasps. Slowly,the hand released her, and she spun around to face her captor. To her surprise, it was a young man,his face partially hidden in the shadows. His eyes were intense,his expression grim.

"Who are you?" Eliza demanded, her voice low and fierce. "What do you want?"

"My name is William," he said, glancing around nervously. "I serve Lord Rochford,but I am not loyal to him.I am loyal to you."

Eliza frowned, her mind racing. "Why?"

"Because I know what you're trying to do," William said quietly. "I've seen you,overheard your conversations. You're trying to protect Mistress Boleyn."

Eliza stomach twisted. How much did this man know? And could she trust him?

"I don't know what you're talking about," she said carefully.

William shook his head. "Don't play games with me. I'm on your side. But you're in danger. Cromwell is watching you, and there are others who would see you silenced. You need to be more careful."

Eliza felt a surge of fear. Had Cromwell sent this man to trap her, to test her loyalty?

"Why should I believe you?" she asked,her voice trembling.

William sighed. "You have no reason to trust me, I know that. But if you continue as you are,you will be caught. And if that happens, Anne will fall. You're not just putting yourself at risk,you're putting her at risk too."

Eliza,s mind raced. She had known the risks,but hearing them spoken aloud made them all too real.

"What do you suggest?" she asked finally.

William glanced around again,his expression tense. "Meet me tomorrow, at dawn,in the old chapel. I'll explain everything then. But for now, you need to go back inside. Act normal. Pretend this conversation never happened."

Eliza hesitated,every instinct screaming at her to flee. But something in William's eyes,something sincere and desperate,held her back.

"Fine," she said, her voice steady. "I'll meet you. But if this is a trap"

"It's not," William said quickly. "I swear. Now go, before someone sees us."

Eliza turned and hurried back toward the Palace,her heart racing. As she slipped back into the banquet hall,she cast a quick glance around, searching for Cromwell. He was still there,his gaze distant as he spoke with another courtier.

Had he seen her slip away? Was he already planning her downfall?

Eliza took a deep breath, forcing herself to calm down. She had made a choice,and now she would have to see it through. Tomorrow, she would meet William and find out what he knew. And then she would decide her next move. For now, she would play her part,smile and nod,and pray that she could navigate the treacherous waters she had found herself in.

As the night wore on,Eliza,s resolve hardened.

She had come to this time to understand Anne Boleyn,to see her as she truly was. But now,she was caught up in a deadly game, where the stakes were higher than she had ever imagined.

She could only hope that she was strong enough to survive it.

Chapter Eight: Unmasking the Game

Dawn broke over the Palace grounds, casting light over the turrets and spires of the majestic court. Eliza wrapped her cloak tightly around her as she made her way through the deserted corridors. The air was crisp, filled with the scent of dew and the faint chirping of birds. She moved quickly,her heart pounding with anticipation and dread. The encounter with William last night had left her shaken,his warnings echoing in her mind.

The old chapel stood at the edge of the Palace grounds,a relic from a bygone era,now rarely used. Its stone walls were covered in ivy,and its small, stained-glass windows were muted in the early morning light. Eliza paused at the entrance,her gaze sweeping over the silent building. She couldn't shake the fear that this was a trap and that Cromwell had set her up and she was walking into her own undoing.

Taking a deep breath,she pushed the door open and slipped inside. The chapel was dim and cool,the air thick with the scent of incense and candle wax. The early morning sunlight filtering through the stained glass,casting a kaleidoscope of colours on the stone floor. It was empty, save for a lone figure standing near the altar.

William turned as she approached, his expression tense, but relieved. He looked younger in the soft light, the hard edges of his face softened by the flickering glow of the candles.

"You came," he said quietly, his voice low.

Eliza nodded, her gaze steady. "You asked me to.Now, tell me why."

William glanced around, as if expecting someone to leap out from the shadows. When he was satisfied they were alone, he stepped closer.

"Anne Boleyn has many enemies," he began, his voice barely above a whisper. "But none more dangerous than Thomas Cromwell. He's clever, ruthless, and utterly determined to control the King. He sees Anne as a threat to his influence,and he won't stop until she is destroyed."

Eliza,s heart clenched. She had suspected Cromwell's intentions,but hearing it confirmed was chilling. "What does he plan to do?"

William hesitated, his gaze flickering over her face as if gauging her reaction. "He's gathering evidence—real or fabricated,it doesn't matter—to bring her down. He's manipulating the king,planting seeds of doubt. It's subtle now,but he's building his case. When the time is right, he'll strike."

Eliza swallowed hard, her mind racing. "And what about me?

Why did you warn me?"

William's expression softened slightly. "Because I know you care for her. You're trying to protect her,just as I am. And because I can see you're not from here."

Eliza,s blood ran cold. She took a step back,her pulse thundering in her ears. "What do you mean?"

He raised his hands, palms outward, in a gesture of peace. "I don't know how or why, but I've seen things— heard you speak of things no one in this time could know. You're different, Eliza. I don't know where you're from,but you're not like the others."

Panic surged through her. Had she been so careless? Had her cover been blown? "You're mistaken," she said, her voice trembling. "I'm just—"

"Don't," William interrupted gently. "You don't have to lie to me. I'm not your enemy."

Eliza stared at him, her mind whirling. How much did he know? And could she trust him?

"I don't understand," she said finally, her voice breaking. "Why are you helping me?"

William's expression turned grim. "Because if Cromwell suspects you're not who you say you are,you'll be in as much danger as Anne. He'll use you against her. And I can't let that happen."

Eliza took a deep breath,struggling to steady herself.
"What do you want me to do?"
"Be careful," William said urgently. "Watch what you
say,who you trust. Stay close to Anne,but don't draw
attention to yourself. And if you hear anything,anything at
all,that could help us,you must tell me."
Eliza nodded slowly. "And what will you do?"
"I'll keep my eyes and ears open," he replied. "I have a
few allies,people who feel the same way I do. We're not
many,but we're loyal. Together, we might be able to slow
Cromwell down,buy Anne some time."
Eliza felt a flicker of hope. It was slim,but it was
something.
"Thank you, William," she said quietly.
He nodded, his expression earnest. "Just be careful,Eliza.
Cromwell is dangerous,and he doesn't play fair. He'll use
whatever he can to get what he wants."

They stood in silence for a moment,the weight of their
predicament hanging heavy between them. Then,with a
final nod,William turned and slipped out of the
chapel,leaving Eliza alone with her thoughts.
She sank onto one of the worn wooden pews, her mind
racing.
What had she gotten herself into?
She had come to this time to learn,to understand,not to
change history. But now she was caught in the middle of
a deadly game,with stakes far higher than she had ever
imagined.
If Cromwell succeeded in bringing Anne down,the
repercussions would be devastating,not just for Anne,but
for the entire kingdom.
Henry's wrath would be terrible,and those who had
supported Anne would be swept away in the storm. Eliza

shuddered at the thought of what might happen to George Boleyn,to the other courtiers,even to Henry himself.
And then there was Anne. Proud,defiant,brilliant Anne. Eliza,s heart ached at the thought of what awaited her. She had seen the histories in old parchment,read the accounts of Anne's final days,her trial,her execution. The injustice of it all burned in her chest.
Could she really stand by and watch it happen?
But what could she do? She was just one person,trapped in a time, not her own,without allies or resources. If she tried to intervene,she could make things even worse.

But doing nothing felt like a betrayal. To Anne,to herself,to everything she believed in.
Eliza rose,her resolve hardening.
She would do what she could,as carefully and quietly as possible.
She would watch and listen, and if she could find a way to help, she would take it.
With a final glance around the silent chapel,she slipped out into the morning light,her mind set. Whatever the future held,she would face it. For Anne,and for the sake of the history she loved.
As she made her way back to the palace, her thoughts turned to Anne's Coronation . It would be a grand affair,a spectacle of power and glory. But beneath the glittering surface,the court was a cauldron of intrigue and danger. Eliza knew that she would have to tread carefully,navigate the treacherous waters of court politics with skill and subtlety. And all the while,she would have to hide her true identity,her knowledge of what was to come.
It would be a delicate dance,one misstep could be fatal.
But Eliza was determined for William,s sake and her,s.

The man named William,whom Eliza had met with,in the church,was William Brereton. He is a prominent member of Henry VIII's court and a Gentleman of the Privy Chamber. Known for his influence and connections,Brereton is part of the king's inner circle,holding significant power and responsibility. However, his ambitions and associations make him a dangerous figure to cross.

Eliza thinks about the visit with William in the church as she walks back and realises that there are complex and often perilous web of loyalties and rivalries within the Tudor court.William,s presence in the church, seemingly coincidental,underscores the constant surveillance and intrigue surrounding Anne Boleyn and her supporters. William's role suggests to Eliza that there are tensions brewing beneath the surface,as different factions vie for power and influence,are foreshadowing the tragic events that will eventually unfold and it makes her shiver as she thinks about it all.

Chapter Nine: The Crown and the Cradle

Spring dawned with a flurry of activity and anticipation at court. The Palace buzzed with excitement,for the long-awaited day had arrived: Anne Boleyn would be crowned Queen of England. Whispers of her secret marriage to Henry had finally been confirmed, though only to a select few. Now,her rising status would be publicly cemented,her place beside the King solidified.

But beneath the gilded façade of the festivities,a deeper,more private joy blossomed,that Anne was carrying the King,s child. The prospect of an heir lent an urgency to the coronation,as if all of England were holding its breath, waiting for this new chapter in their history to unfold.

Eliza observed the court's frenzied preparations with a mix of fascination and anxiety. She moved among the courtiers and servants, carefully maintaining her cover while keeping a watchful eye on Anne. As Eliza watched the final fittings of Anne's beautiful coronation robes, she couldn't help,but notice the subtle curve of Anne's stomach beneath the layers of rich fabric.

"How are you feeling,Mistress" Eliza asked quietly as they stood alone in Anne's private chambers,the noise of the bustling court muted by the heavy wooden door.

Anne turned, her face glowing with a happiness that seemed almost otherworldly. "Tired, but content," she admitted, her hand resting gently on her belly. "It has all happened so quickly, Eliza. One moment, I was merely the King,s love, and now…" She trailed off, her eyes distant. "Now I am his wife and soon,God willing, the mother of his heir."

Eliza smiled, though concern shadowed her gaze. "You are more than that,Mistress. You will be the Queen of England and a good Queen. No one can take that from you now and your name will be remembered for generations."
Anne never said anything when Eliza called her by her first name sometimes by accident,just accepted that Eliza had become so much more than a lady in waiting.
She had become a trusted friend and some one whom she cared for very much.

Anne's expression faltered for a brief moment, a flicker of anxiety passing over her features. "You think so? I sometimes wonder. There are still many who oppose me,who whisper that I have usurped Queen Katherine's place."

Eliza took a step closer, her voice firm. "You have earned this place, Anne. Do not let anyone make you doubt that."

Anne nodded, but her smile was strained. "I am trying to be brave,to be the Queen that Henry needs. But this—this child is everything. If I bear him a son,no one will be able to question my position."

There it was, the unspoken fear that had haunted Anne from the moment she had first captured Henry's attention. Eliza,s heart ached for her. She understood the pressure,the immense weight of expectation resting on Anne's slender shoulders.

"Everything will be fine," Eliza said softly. "You are strong,and your child will be strong too."

Anne squeezed her hand in silent thanks. "I must believe that," she murmured. "For now, I must focus on the Coronation. It is not just for me, but for our child's future."

Eliza nodded,her thoughts drifting back to the history she knew and what she wanted so much to tell Anne—the tragic story of Anne's short reign and her ultimate downfall. But standing here, in this moment, it was hard to reconcile that bleak future with the radiant and beautiful woman before her. Anne was so full of hope and determination, so fiercely alive. The idea that all this joy could be snatched away seemed almost impossible and absolutely heartbreaking.

The day of the Coronation dawned clear and bright, the sky,a brilliant blue overhead, as London's streets filled with throngs of spectators. Banners fluttered from every window,and the air was thick with the scent of flowers and the sound of church bells pealing in celebration.

Anne's procession to Westminster Abbey was a spectacle of grandeur and opulence. She rode in a litter draped in cloth of gold,her black hair loose beneath a smaller jewelled crown that glinted in the sunshine. Her gown, a shimmering creation of white silk and silver thread, seemed to catch the sunlight and hold it,making her appear almost ethereal. Around her neck a magnificent necklace of red rubies and diamonds sparkled,a gift from Henry to mark her ascension.

As Eliza followed in the Queen,s retinue, she couldn't help,but marvel at the sight before her. The people lined the streets,cheering and waving, their faces alight with curiosity and excitement. Yet, there were also those whose expressions were dark, their mouths set in grim lines. Loyalists to Katherine,no doubt, or those who still harboured doubts about Anne's legitimacy.

Inside the Abbey, the atmosphere was reverent,charged with a sense of history in the making. The choir's voices soared,filling the cavernous space with hymns that seemed to echo through the centuries,The heralds blew their trumpets in reverence as Anne moved gracefully down the aisle,her steps measured, her head held high. But Eliza, walking just behind her, could see the slight stiffness in her shoulders, the way her hand occasionally brushed her belly, as if seeking reassurance.

The ceremony itself was a blur of ritual and pageantry. Archbishop Cranmer anointed Anne with holy oil, his hands steady as he intoned the ancient prayers. Then,with deliberate care,with the smaller crown now removed, he placed the crown of St. Edward upon her head, its weight a visible burden as well as an honour. For a moment,there was silence,the entire assembly holding its breath.

And then, the applause broke out, filling the Abbey like a wave. Anne rose,her eyes bright with unshed tears, her smile radiant. Eliza felt her own throat tighten with emotion. This was it—the pinnacle of Anne's triumph. She was Queen, crowned and anointed,her position secured by the might of the church and the will of the King and Eliza had watched every sacred moment of it with tears streaming down her face with joy still unable to believe what she was witnessing in real life.
This was a time traveller's dream and Eliza swore that for the rest of her life,she would never forget her time or her glimpses of events that happened,of her time in this world of Tudor England.

As they left the Abbey, the sun was high in the sky, casting a warm, golden light over the city. The crowds were even larger now, their cheers louder, more fervent. Anne waved from her litter, her smile never faltering, though Eliza could see the strain behind her eyes. The weight of the crown, combined with the demands of her pregnancy, was taking its toll.

Back at the Palace, a grand banquet awaited, the tables laden with delicacies and the finest wines. Eliza moved through the throng of courtiers and diplomats,her eyes always on Anne. The Queen sat at the head of the table next to the King,her posture regal, her smile fixed as she accepted the endless toasts and tributes. But beneath the surface, Eliza could see her exhaustion, the way her hand rested protectively over her stomach.

As the evening wore on, Anne finally rose, her voice clear and strong as she addressed the assembled guests. "Today is a day of great joy, not just for me and his Majesty,the King,but for all of England," she declared. "I am honoured to be your Queen, and I vow to serve this realm with all my heart. My husband, your King, has given me the greatest gift of all—the chance to bear his child. Together, we will lead England into a new era of peace and prosperity."

The applause that followed was thunderous, but Eliza,s heart clenched. She knew the path ahead would not be as simple or as smooth as Anne hoped. There were still too many enemies lurking in the shadows, too many threats to her hard-won crown.

As the guests began to depart from the Palace at the end of the evening,Eliza made her way to Anne's side. The Queen's face was pale,her smile wavering. "You need to rest,Anne," Eliza said quietly. "You've done more than enough today."

Anne nodded, her hand trembling as she reached for Eliza,s arm. "Yes, I suppose I should. It has been overwhelming."

Together, they made their way to Anne's private chambers,the Palace corridors quiet and dim in the fading light. Once inside, Anne sank onto a cushioned chair, her head resting against the back. "I feel as if I've run a thousand miles," she whispered, her eyes closed.

"You have carried the weight of a kingdom today," Eliza said softly. "It's no wonder you're exhausted."

Anne's hand moved to her belly, a small, contented smile playing on her lips. "And more than that. I wonder sometimes if this child knows what awaits it. If it can sense the hopes and fears I carry."

Eliza knelt beside her, taking Anne's hand in hers. "Your child will be strong and brave, just like its mother. And you really will be the most wonderful Queen, Anne.I truly believe that."

Anne's eyes fluttered open, and she looked down at Eliza, her gaze filled with gratitude and something else— something softer, more vulnerable. "Thank you, Eliza. You have been a true friend to me. I don't know what I would do without you."

Eliza felt a lump form in her throat. She squeezed Anne's hand gently. "You'll never have to find out, Anne. I'm here,always."

The door opened and there stood the King,come to spend the night with his Queen and Eliza curtsied and left the room

As the candles flickered in the corridor and the shadows deepened around her, Eliza made a silent vow. She would protect Anne and her child,no matter what it took. She would stand by her, through every challenge and every danger.

The road ahead would not be easy, but Eliza knew she could not—would not—let Anne face it alone.

Chapter Ten: The Birth of Hope

The summer heat hung heavy in the air as Anne retreated to the relative seclusion of Hampton Court, her belly swollen with the promise of a new life. Anticipation crackled through the court like a distant storm as the final days of Anne's pregnancy drew near. The child she carried was not just a future prince or princess; it was the culmination of Anne's ambitions, the fulfilment of Henry's dreams, and the hope of the entire Tudor dynasty.

Eliza,ever by Anne's side, witnessed the queen's moments of anxiety and joy as the days crept closer. The Palace,with its vast halls and manicured gardens, seemed to pulse with a kind of breathless expectation. Courtiers whispered and speculated, placing discreet wagers on whether the child would be the long-awaited male heir.

But for Anne, the world narrowed to the chambers she occupied, her days and nights filled with the discomfort of her pregnancy and the haunting uncertainty of what was to come. Despite the bravado she displayed to Henry and the court, Eliza knew the doubts that plagued her friend.

"It will be a boy," Anne would say resolutely, her voice strong but her eyes betraying a flicker of fear. "It must be."

Eliza would offer her a reassuring smile. "Boy or girl, it will be healthy and strong, just like its mother."

Anne laughed at that remark, the sound slightly strained. "Oh, Eliza, you are too kind. But I know the stakes. This child will determine everything—for me, for Henry, for England."

Eliza had no reply to that. The weight of history pressed upon her shoulders, for she knew what Anne did not— how this chapter would end, how desperately Anne would try to give Henry the son he desired, and how, ultimately, it would not be enough. But she kept those dark thoughts buried deep, offering only support and companionship to the Queen,she had come to care for so deeply.

The night of the birth arrived with a suddenness that startled them all. Anne had been restless throughout the day, her hand often straying to her belly, her face pale beneath the glow of candlelight. Eliza had been by her side, offering sips of water and whispered words of comfort, when Anne's first cry of pain split the air.

Panic and excitement rippled through the palace. Midwives and physicians were summoned, and the Queen was carefully helped to her bed, her face taut with concentration and fear. Eliza remained close, her heart pounding in her chest as she watched Anne struggle through the pain,her breaths coming in sharp, uneven gasps.

"It's happening," Anne whispered, her voice trembling. "God,Eliza, I'm so frightened."

Eliza grasped Anne's hand, her own heart aching with the intensity of her friend's fear. "You're going to be fine, Anne," she whispered.."You are strong. You can do this."

The hours that followed were a blur of pain and effort, Anne's cries mingling with the soft murmurs of the midwives and the anxious shuffling of servants outside the door. Eliza never left her side, holding Anne's hand through every contraction, wiping the sweat from her brow, whispering encouragements even as her own nerves frayed.

And then, just as dawn began to creep over the horizon, it happened. With one final, exhausted push, Anne's body arched, and the room filled with the sharp, clear cry of a newborn.

"It's a girl," the midwife announced, her voice both triumphant and tentative. She held the tiny, wriggling form up for Anne to see, and Eliza felt her breath catch at the sight.

Anne's face, streaked with sweat and tears, broke into a radiant smile as she reached out for her daughter. "A girl," she breathed, her voice thick with emotion. "My beautiful daughter ."

The midwife carefully placed the infant in Anne's arms, and for a moment, the world seemed to hold its breath. Anne gazed down at her child, her expression a mixture of awe and adoration. The baby's skin was flushed and pink, her eyes scrunched tightly shut, her tiny fists waving in the air as if already grasping for life.

"Hello, my little Elizabeth," Anne whispered, her voice trembling with love and relief. "You are perfect."

Eliza felt tears prick her eyes as she watched Anne cradle her daughter, her joy so fierce and pure that it seemed to light up the entire room. She knew that in this moment, nothing else mattered to Anne—no court intrigue, no political maneuvering, no fear of the future. There was only this: a mother and her child, a bond as ancient and unbreakable as time itself.

But outside the room, the world continued to turn. News of the birth spread quickly through the palace, and with it came the inevitable whispers of disappointment. Henry had been hoping for a son, an heir to secure his legacy and the future of the Tudor line. A daughter, while still a blessing, was not the triumph he had so desperately sought.

When King Henry entered the room, his expression was carefully controlled, a smile playing at the edges of his mouth. He approached the bed slowly, his eyes fixed on the tiny bundle in Anne's arms.

"She is beautiful," he said softly, his voice betraying none of the disappointment,Eliza knew he must be feeling. He reached out a hand, touching his daughter's cheek with surprising gentleness.

Anne's eyes shone with gratitude as she looked up at him. "Thank you, Henry. She will be everything we hoped for, I promise.Her name is Elizabeth after your mother"

Henry's smile tightened slightly, but he nodded. "I know she will, Anne. And there will be time for more children. Time for a son."

Eliza.s heart clenched at the words, the unspoken pressure they carried. But Anne only smiled, her gaze never leaving her daughter's face.

"Yes," she said softly. "There will be time."

The christening of Princess Elizabeth was held a couple of weeks later in the beautiful chapel at Hampton Court, a ceremony filled with both grandeur and a strange, poignant intimacy. The chapel itself was a masterpiece of gothic splendour , its high, vaulted ceilings adorned with intricate carvings and stained glass windows that cast jewel-toned light across the assembled guests.

Anne, now recovered from childbirth was dressed in a gown of deep crimson velvet trimmed with ermine, looked every inch the proud and loving mother as she carried Elizabeth to the altar. The baby,swathed in delicate lace and silks, seemed almost too small and fragile in her mother's arms, her tiny face peaceful as she slept.

Henry stood beside them, his expression calm and composed, his hand resting lightly on Anne's arm. The court watched with rapt attention as the Archbishop of Canterbury performed the ancient rites and put holy water from the font on the baby's head,his voice echoing through the chapel as he blessed the child and named her Elizabeth.

Eliza, standing among the ladies of the court, felt a swell of emotion as she watched the ceremony unfold. There was something profoundly moving about the sight of this tiny, helpless baby at the center of so much hope and expectation. Elizabeth was more than just a child; she was a symbol of promise, a new beginning for the Tudor dynasty.

At the moment the Archbishop had anointed Elizabeth with holy water, Anne's eyes filled with tears. Eliza knew that in this moment, all of Anne's fears and doubts were swept away by a love so fierce and unconditional that it seemed to light her from within. She looked at her daughter as if she were the most precious treasure in the world, as if no future heartbreak or disappointment could ever diminish the joy of this moment.

When the ceremony ended, the royal family turned to face the court, and a ripple of applause swept through the gathered guests. Anne's smile was radiant as she looked out at the sea of faces including her parents,Thomas and Elizabeth Boleyn,her brother George, her daughter held securely in her arms. For this brief, shining moment, all the struggles and sacrifices she had endured seemed worth it.

But Eliza could not shake the sense of unease that coiled in her chest. She knew that this happiness, this fleeting peace, was only the calm before the storm. There were too many forces at play, too many enemies waiting in the shadows. And as much as she wanted to believe in the promise of this new beginning, she could not forget the history, she knew all too well.

After the ceremony, a lavish banquet was held in the Great Hall, the tables groaning under the weight of rich foods and fine wines. Eliza watched as Henry and Anne received the congratulations of their guests, their smiles bright, their laughter easy. But she also saw the glances exchanged between the courtiers, the subtle undercurrent of tension that ran beneath the surface of the festivities.

As the evening wore on, Eliza found herself standing alone by one of the tall windows, looking out over the darkened gardens. The air was cool and fragrant, the sky above a deep, star-strewn blue. She closed her eyes, letting the quiet calm her racing thoughts.

"You seem lost in thought."

Eliza turned to find Anne standing beside her, Elizabeth cradled in her arms. The queen's face was soft in the candlelight, her eyes still bright with the joy of the day.

"I was just thinking how beautiful everything is," Eliza said, forcing a smile. "And how happy I am for you, Anne."

Anne's smile widened, but there was a hint of sadness in her eyes. "Thank you,Eliza. It means so much to me to have you here,sharing this with me."

Eliza hesitated, then reached out to gently touch Elizabeth's tiny hand. "She is perfect, Anne.Truly,...My real name is Elizabeth,but everyone calls me Eliza"

Anne's gaze softened as she looked down at her daughter. "Yes, she is. And I will love her with all my heart, no matter what the future holds and how wonderful that your name is Elizabeth too."

Chapter Eleven: Hope and Ambition

As autumn settled over England, the court continued its celebrations, and Princess Elizabeth quickly became the apple of Anne's eye. The Palace halls were filled with the sweet coos of the newborn, her laughter echoing like a melody that momentarily softened even the most hardened of courtiers. For Anne, every day brought new wonders. Elizabeth's tiny fingers wrapping around hers, the first time her daughter's eyes opened to the world— each moment was a treasure, a victory over the shadows that loomed ever-present.

Yet, despite the joy of new motherhood, Anne was acutely aware of the weight of expectation that still rested on her shoulders. Henry's desire for a male heir was like a spectre haunting every corner of the Palace. He was affectionate with his new daughter, but it was clear to all that his mind was set on what would come next. Another pregnancy. A son. A prince to secure his legacy.

One evening, as Eliza sat with Anne in her chambers,the Queen voiced the fears that had been gnawing at her heart.

"Do you think I've failed him, Eliza?" Anne's voice was soft, almost lost in the crackle of the fire. She cradled Elizabeth gently, her fingers tracing the curve of her daughter's cheek. "Do you think he regrets everything he's sacrificed to be with me?"

Eliza shook her head, her heart aching at the uncertainty in Anne's eyes. "You have not failed, Anne. Elizabeth is healthy and strong. She will be a great queen one day."

"But it's not enough, is it?" Anne's gaze turned to the flames, her expression distant. "He needs a son. The court, the kingdom, they all expect it. And what if I can't give him that?"

"You will," Eliza said, more forcefully than she intended. "You will, Anne. You are strong, and you will hopefully give him the heir he desires."

Anne smiled faintly,but there was no joy in it. "I hope you're right. For both our sakes."

The pressure on Anne to conceive again was palpable. It was not just Henry's expectation, but also the whispers of the courtiers, the murmurings of those who had never accepted Anne as queen. They watched her every move, scrutinising her health, her interactions with the King, waiting for any sign that another child was on the way.

Despite the constant scrutiny, Anne remained as involved as ever in the affairs of the court. She had always been more than just a consort—she was Henry's partner in all things, his confidante, his political ally. She attended council meetings, advised on foreign policy, and made her presence felt in every decision that shaped the kingdom. It was a role she had fought hard for, and she would not relinquish it lightly.

But the strain was taking its toll. Eliza could see the fatigue in Anne's eyes, the way her shoulders slumped when she thought no one was watching. There were days when Anne's temper flared, sharp and sudden, her frustration boiling over in a torrent of angry words. She would snap at her ladies-in-waiting, at the courtiers who sought her favor, even at Eliza herself.

"I'm sorry," Anne would say afterward, her voice thick with regret. "I just—sometimes it's all too much."

Eliza would simply nod, offering what comfort she could. She knew better than anyone the pressure Anne was under, the expectations that threatened to crush her. And yet, there was so little she could do to ease her friend's burden. Eliza was just a witness to it all and that was the hardest thing.

In the midst of this turmoil, Henry's attention seemed to waver. He was often away on hunts or involved in state matters, his visits to Anne's chambers growing less frequent. When he did see her, his affection was tinged with a kind of restless impatience, as if he were waiting for something that had yet to come.

One evening, as Eliza stood in the shadows of Anne's chamber, helping the Queen prepare for bed, Henry arrived unexpectedly. His presence filled the room, his gaze intense as he looked at his wife and daughter.

"Leave us," he commanded softly, his eyes never leaving Anne's face. The servants and ladies-in-waiting, including Eliza, hurried to obey, slipping from the room as silently as ghosts.

Eliza hesitated in the doorway, her heart pounding. She knew she should leave, but something in the tension between the king and queen held her rooted to the spot.

"Eliza," Anne's voice cut through the silence, gentle but firm. "It's all right. Go."

With a nod, Eliza turned and left, the door closing softly behind her. She lingered outside, her ear pressed to the wood, straining to catch the murmur of voices within.

"Anne," she heard Henry say, his tone low and urgent. "You know how much I love you. You know what I've done to make you my Queen. But the future of our realm rests on this. We need a son, Anne."

Anne's reply was too quiet for Eliza to hear, but she could imagine the pain in her friend's eyes, the fear that must be gripping her heart.

"I will give you a son, Henry," Anne's voice rose, fierce and determined. "I will not fail you."

There was a pause, then the sound of Henry's heavy sigh. "I know you will try, my love. But it must be soon. We cannot wait forever."

Eliza stepped back, her heart aching for Anne. She knew that the Queen's determination was unyielding,but so was

Henry's desire for a male heir. It was a battle Anne could not afford to lose, and the stakes were higher than ever.

The following weeks saw Anne retreat from the public eye, her appearances at court becoming less frequent as she focused on her health and on spending time with Elizabeth. Henry, meanwhile, threw himself into his duties, his absences from Hampton Court growing longer and more frequent. Eliza could sense the distance growing between them, a gap that neither seemed able—or willing—to bridge.

One cold, crisp morning, Eliza found Anne in the royal nursery, holding Elizabeth close as she gazed out the window. The baby cooed softly, her tiny hands reaching for her mother's face, her eyes bright and curious.

"Look at her," Anne murmured as Eliza approached. "So innocent, so full of life. She has no idea of the world she's been born into, the expectations that will one day rest on her shoulders."

Eliza placed a gentle hand on Anne's arm. "She is happy, Anne. And she is loved. That is enough for now."

Anne turned to look at Eliza, her eyes shining with unshed tears. "But will it be enough for Henry? For the court? For the kingdom?"

Before Eliza could reply, the door to the nursery opened, and Henry strode in. His presence filled the room, and for a moment, he seemed to bring with him the cold bite of the winter air outside.Eliza curtsied and left the room.

"Henry," Anne said, her voice softening as she held Elizabeth out to him. "Look at your daughter. Isn't she beautiful?"

Henry's gaze flicked to the child, a faint smile touching his lips. "Yes, she is. She will be a fine princess."

He took Elizabeth from Anne's arms, holding her awkwardly for a moment before handing her back. "But you know what we must do, Anne. You must conceive again,and soon."

Anne's face tightened, but she nodded. "I know, Henry.I will do everything in my power."

Henry's expression softened, and he reached out to cup Anne's cheek. "I have faith in you, Anne. You are my queen, my love. We will have our son."

He kissed her forehead, then turned and left, his footsteps echoing down the corridor.

Anne stood there for a long moment, holding Elizabeth close, her face a mask of conflicting emotions. Then she turned to Eliza who had now returned, her voice trembling. "I will give him a son, Eliza. I must."

Eliza nodded,her heart heavy. She knew that Anne's resolve was unbreakable, but she also knew the uncertainty that lay ahead. For all her strength and determination, Anne was at the mercy of forces beyond her control—forces that could either elevate her to untold heights or dash her hopes to pieces.

As the days grew shorter and winter tightened its grip on England, Anne threw herself into the task of fulfilling Henry's wishes. She observed every piece of advice given by the physicians, followed every superstition and remedy. Eliza watched, a silent witness to Anne's quiet desperation, her unwavering resolve.

And yet, beneath the surface of hope and ambition, Eliza could feel the currents of tension pulling at them all. The court was a place of whispers and shadows, of alliances and betrayals. And as much as Eliza wished she could protect her friend from the dangers that lurked around every corner, she knew that the greatest danger of all lay within the palace walls itself—the relentless pressure to produce a son.

But for now, in the warm glow of the nursery, with Elizabeth's laughter filling the air, there was still hope. And as Anne kissed her daughter's forehead and whispered promises of a bright future, Eliza prayed that this fragile peace would last, that the joy of this moment would not be shattered by the weight of the crown.

Chapter Twelve: Tensions at Court

As winter's chill seeped through the thick walls of Hampton Court, the tension at court became almost palpable. Anne's efforts to conceive again were well-known, and every lady-in-waiting, every servant, every noble seemed to be holding their breath, waiting for any sign that the Queen might be with child once more.

Eliza, ever observant, noticed the way Anne's hand would sometimes rest on her stomach, as if willing a life to begin there. There was a quiet desperation in her eyes that she could not disguise, even from her closest confidante.

Meanwhile, the court was rife with speculation. Rumours swirled like the snow outside—rumours that Anne was losing the Kings favour , that he was already looking elsewhere for the son she had failed to give him. Eliza did her best to shield Anne from the worst of it, but there was no hiding the whispers that echoed through the palace halls.

One afternoon, as Eliza accompanied Anne on a walk through the Palace gardens, the Queen turned to her, her expression a mix of determination and fear.

"I feel as though I am walking on a knife's edge, Eliza," she said quietly, her breath misting in the cold air. "Every day I am scrutinised, judged. The courtiers look at me as though they are waiting for me to fail."

Eliza placed a comforting hand on her friend's arm. "You have not failed, Anne. You are the Queen, and you have given Henry a beautiful daughter. As I have told you, Elizabeth will be a great Queen one day, I am certain of it."

"But it's not enough, is it?" Anne's voice was bitter. "A daughter is not enough. If I cannot give him a son, all of this—everything I have sacrificed—will be for nothing."

Eliza knew there was no easy comfort she could offer. The pressure on Anne was immense, and it was not just Henry's expectations she had to contend with, but the entire kingdom's. The stakes were higher than ever, and the consequences of failure unthinkable.

As they returned to the Palace chilled through because of the snow, Eliza noticed the way the courtiers watched Anne. Their eyes followed her every move, their expressions a mixture of curiosity, envy, and disdain. Anne's position was precarious, and they all knew it. There were those who had never accepted her as queen, who still saw her as the woman who had supplanted the beloved Katherine of Aragon. To them, Anne's every misstep was proof that she was unworthy of the crown.

Among those watching was Jane Seymour, a lady-in-waiting who had recently caught Henry's eye. Eliza had seen the way the King,s gaze lingered on Jane, the way his expression softened when she was near. It was a subtle but undeniable shift, and it made Eliza,s heart ache for her friend,Anne.

Anne, too, had noticed. One evening, as they sat together in Anne's chambers, she spoke of it, her voice tight with anger and fear.

"He looks at her the way he used to look at me," she said, her hands clenched in her lap. "I see it, Eliza. I see the way his eyes follow her, the way he smiles when she speaks."

Eliza tried to offer reassurance. "Henry loves you, Anne. He has done so much to be with you, to make you his Queen. He will not abandon you so easily."

Anne shook her head, her eyes dark with worry. "But what if I can't give him a son? What then? He is a King, Eliza. His loyalty is to his throne, to his legacy. And if he believes I cannot give him an heir—" She broke off, her voice choked with emotion.

"He will not abandon you," Eliza said firmly, though she could not silence the doubts that whispered in her own heart. "You are his wife, the mother of his daughter. You are his partner in everything."

But even as she spoke the words, Eliza knew how fragile Anne's position was. Henry's love was powerful, but so too was his ambition, his desire for a male heir to secure his dynasty. If Anne could not give him that, would his affection be enough to hold them together?

The months passed in a blur of hope and anxiety. Anne's every movement was watched, every word scrutinised for hints of a pregnancy that never came. The strain was beginning to show. She became thinner, her once-vibrant beauty dulled by sleepless nights and the constant pressure of the court's expectations.

One evening, as they sat by the fire in Anne's chambers, Eliza finally voiced the question that had been haunting her.

"Anne, what will you do if—if it doesn't happen? If you can't—"

Anne's eyes flashed with a mixture of defiance and desperation. "I will not fail, Eliza. I cannot fail. I will give him a son, whatever it takes."

Eliza nodded, though her heart was heavy. She knew how determined Anne was, but she also knew how much was beyond her control. And as much as she wanted to believe that everything would work out, the shadows of doubt were impossible to ignore.

As the court prepared for the coming spring, the tension only grew. Henry's absences became more frequent, and when he was at Hampton Court, he was often seen in Jane Seymour's company. Anne's temper flared more often, her frustration and fear manifesting in sharp words and sudden tears.

Eliza did her best to support her friend, but she could feel the distance growing between them, a chasm of fear and uncertainty that neither of them could bridge. Anne was withdrawing into herself, her once-boundless energy and ambition tempered by the harsh reality of her situation.

And all the while, the court watched, waiting for the next twist in the story of the King and his Queen. Waiting to see if Anne would succeed or if she would fall, like so many before her, to the relentless demands of the crown.

One day, as Eliza walked through the palace gardens, she overheard a conversation between two courtiers. They spoke in hushed tones, their words sharp with disdain.

"She'll never give him a son," one of them said. "It's only a matter of time before he sets her aside, like he did the last one."

The other laughed, a cruel sound that made Eliza,s blood boil. "And who will take her place? That Seymour girl? The king seems quite taken with her."

Eliza felt a surge of anger, but she forced herself to remain calm. Confronting them would do no good; it would only draw attention, make things worse for Anne. But the words lingered in her mind, a bitter echo of the doubts that had been growing in her own heart.

That evening, as she sat with Anne in her chambers, she couldn't keep silent any longer.

"Anne, you must be careful," she said, her voice low and urgent. "There are those at court who are waiting for you to fail. They will use any excuse to turn Henry against you."

Anne looked up, her eyes fierce. "I know, Eliza. I am not blind to what is happening. But I will not be defeated. I will give him a son, and then they will have no power over me."

Eliza wished she could share her friend's certainty, but the doubts remained. She could see the toll the pressure was taking on Anne, the way her spirit seemed to dim a little more each day. And she could see the way Henry's gaze lingered on Jane Seymour, the way his smile softened when she was near.

As spring gave way to summer, the court's anticipation reached a fever pitch. Would the queen finally announce a new pregnancy? Or would Henry's patience run out, his wandering eye settle permanently on another?

Eliza could only watch, a silent witness to the unfolding drama. She had come to this time to learn, to observe, but now she found herself caught up in the story, her heart breaking for her friend, for the Queen, brought up in Hever Castle in Kent who had risked everything and now stood on the brink of losing it all.

And yet, through it all, Anne remained defiant, her spirit unbroken. She held her head high, her eyes bright with determination. She would not be cowed,not by Henry, not by the court, not by the weight of their expectations.

"I am the Queen," she said to Eliza one evening, her voice strong despite the shadows in her eyes. "I have fought for this, and I will not be cast aside. I will give him a son, and I will secure my place. I will not fail."

And as Eliza looked at her friend, Anne,at the fierce light in her eyes, she could only hope that Anne's strength would be enough to see her through the trials that lay ahead.

Chapter Thirteen: The Queen's Determination

The summer heat settled over Hampton Court like a thick blanket, stifling and relentless. It mirrored the growing pressure on Anne Boleyn, whose every movement, every word was scrutinised . Despite her outward defiance, the strain was beginning to show. Her laughter, once vibrant and infectious, had become brittle, her once sparkling eyes clouded with worry.

Eliza watched her closely, her concern deepening with each passing day. Anne was more restless than ever, throwing herself into her duties as Queen with a desperate intensity. She hosted grand feasts, attended council meetings, and oversaw everything about Elizabeth's education in the years to come, all the while maintaining an impeccable façade of confidence and grace. Yet beneath the surface, Eliza could sense the turmoil, the fear that her time was running out.

One afternoon, as they sat in the Queens private chambers, Anne spoke candidly of her fears. Her hands, adorned with glittering rings, twisted anxiously in her lap.

"I feel as though I am living on borrowed time, Eliza," she confessed, her voice barely above a whisper. "The courtiers whisper behind my back, the King grows colder by the day, and all the while I struggle to give him what he so desperately desires."

Eliza reached out, taking Anne's hands in hers. "You are strong,Mistress. You have faced greater challenges than this and overcome them. You are the Queen and you will not be so easily cast aside.You are stronger than you think you are.If I had my way,I would do so much more to help you.To take you and Elizabeth away from the intrigue of court forever to a place where you would not need to worry. I might still do it yet, for it causes me much pain to see you under so much worry and stress"

But Anne's eyes were distant, her thoughts far away. "I wonder sometimes, what will happen to me if I fail. Will I be exiled like Katherine? Or will it be worse?" She shuddered, the unspoken fear hanging heavy in the air.

"Please don't think like that,did you hear what I just said?" Eliza urged once more, squeezing Anne's hands gently." Sorry,Eliza,my mind was elsewhere"So with that Eliza answered "You must focus on your health,on your strength. There is still time, Anne. You can still give him a son."

Anne nodded,but the doubt lingered in her eyes. She had been so certain, so confident that she would bear the King a son,but with each passing month, that certainty had begun to erode, replaced by a gnawing fear that she would never fulfil her promise.

Meanwhile, Henry's attentions had turned more and more towards Jane Seymour. Eliza had seen them together in the gardens, their conversations punctuated by Henry's soft laughter and Jane's shy smiles. It was a cruel irony, Eliza thought, that the King should be so taken with a woman so unlike Anne. Where Anne was fiery and passionate, Jane was demure and submissive, everything Henry now seemed to crave.

One evening, as Eliza and Anne prepared for a banquet in honour of a visiting French ambassador, Anne's frustration boiled over. She stood before her mirror, her ladies fussing over her gown and jewels, but her eyes were stormy, her temper barely contained.

"Why must I endure this farce?" she snapped, her voice sharp. "Why must I smile and nod and play the gracious hostess while my husband flirts with that—girl, right under my nose?"

Eliza dismissed the other ladies with a glance, then turned to Anne, her voice calm and soothing. "You must be patient, Anne. Show them your strength, your resilience. Do not let them see you falter."

"Patience?" Anne laughed bitterly. "I have been patient, Eliza. I have waited and hoped and prayed,but what good has it done me? He is slipping away, and I am powerless to stop it."

"You are not powerless," Eliza insisted, stepping closer. "You are still the Queen. And as long as you hold that title, you have power. Use it, Anne. Show them all why Henry chose you, why he fought for you. Do not let them see you defeated."

Anne took a deep breath, her anger giving way to determination. "You're right. I am the Queen. And I will not be cowed by anyone—not Jane Seymour, not the King, not the entire court either."

The banquet was a grand affair, the hall filled with the glittering elite of England and France. Anne, dressed in a gown of deep crimson velvet, looked every inch the Queen. She moved through the crowd with grace and poise, her head held high, her smile dazzling. Eliza watched with pride as Anne engaged the Ambassador in conversation, her wit and charm on full display.

But beneath the surface, Eliza could see the cracks. There was a tightness to Anne's smile, a flicker of pain in her eyes whenever she glanced at Henry, who sat at the head of the table, his attention focused on Jane Seymour, seated demurely at his side.

After the banquet, as the guests dispersed and the minstrels had finished their music, Anne retreated to her chambers, her mask of confidence slipping away. Eliza followed, her heart aching for her friend.

"He barely looked at me tonight," Anne whispered, sinking in a soft yellow velvet chair, her shoulders slumped. "He was too busy gazing at her, hanging on her every word. What have I done to deserve this?"

"Nothing," Eliza said fiercely, sitting beside her. "You have done nothing wrong, Anne. It is not your fault that he is fickle, that he is so easily swayed. You are his wife, his Queen, and you deserve his respect."

"But it's not respect I need, Eliza. It's love. His love, his faith in me." She looked up, her eyes shining with unshed tears. "How can I fight for him when he no longer believes in me?"

Eliza took her friend's hands, her voice firm. "You fight because you are strong, because you are Anne Boleyn, and you do not give up. You fight because there is still hope, because you are more than just a wife or a Queen—you are a mother, and you have a daughter who needs you."

Anne's gaze softened at the mention of Elizabeth. "Yes, my Elizabeth. She is my greatest joy, my greatest hope."

"Then hold on to that," Eliza urged. "Hold on to her, to your love for her. Let that be your strength, your reason to keep fighting."

Anne nodded, a small, determined smile forming on her lips. "You are right, Eliza. I will not let them break me. I will fight for my daughter, for my family, for everything I have worked so hard to build."

As the days passed, Anne seemed to regain some of her strength. She threw herself into her role as Queen with renewed vigour, overseeing Elizabeth's future education plans, hosting court events, and even involving herself in matters of state. But Eliza could see that the struggle was taking its toll. The tension between Anne and Henry was palpable, their once-passionate love now strained and brittle and Jane Seymour close by which made things even worse.

One afternoon, as Eliza walked through the Palace gardens, she found herself being followed by this other lady. The younger woman, dressed in a simple gown of pale blue, looked almost ethereal in the dappled sunlight.

"Lady Eliza," Jane said softly, her tone polite but guarded. "May I speak with you?"

Eliza inclined her head, though her heart was heavy. "Of course,Lady Jane. What is it you wish to say?" Eliza had to pinch herself as she knew from her history books that, this woman would take Anne,s place and could feel anger burning in her chest

Jane hesitated, her eyes downcast. "I...I know the Queen is troubled. I know she is suffering, and I do not wish to add to her pain."

Eliza studied Jane closely, searching for any hint of malice or deceit and it took all of her resolve not to be nasty. But all she saw was a young woman caught in a situation far beyond her control.

"Then why do you encourage the King,s attentions?" Eliza asked gently. "If you truly care for the Queens well-being, why do you allow yourself to become a pawn in this dangerous game?"

Jane's cheeks flushed, her hands twisting nervously in the folds of her gown. "I do not seek his favour, But what can I do? He is the King, and I am, but a lady-in-waiting. If I refuse him,it will bring ruin upon my family."

Eliza heart softened. She could see that Jane was as much a victim of the court's machinations as Anne. "Be careful,Lady Jane. You are walking a dangerous path,and there are those who would use you to harm the Queen. Do not let yourself be used."

Jane nodded, her eyes filled with a sorrow that seemed beyond her years. "I will try, Lady Eliza. I will try to do what is right."

But as Eliza watched Jane walk away, her heart was heavy with foreboding. She knew that the tides were turning, that forces beyond her control were at work. And no matter how hard Anne fought, no matter how fiercely she clung to her position, there were, according to her history books, some battles that could not be won.

But where could she take Anne to get her away from all of this?,thought Eliza

Back to the future with her.? It was worth a thought and as each day went by,she thought it was the only way to change Anne,s future.

But Eliza had no idea if she could ever get home herself and would she also end her days in a Tudor England ? The tension she was feeling herself was becoming palpable,but she could not show Anne,the heartache she felt for her, because she knew what was coming.

As summer turned to autumn, the tension at court only grew. Henry's attentions to Jane Seymour became more overt, more brazen, while Anne's position grew ever more precarious. Eliza could see the fear in her friend's eyes, the desperation that lurked beneath her defiant façade.

And all the while, the courtiers whispered, their eyes gleaming with anticipation. They sensed that a change was coming, that the Queens time was running out.

But Anne, true to her nature, refused to back down. She continued to fight, to hold her head high, to assert her place at Henry's side. And Eliza,bound by friendship and loyalty, stood by her, offering what support she could, even as the shadows gathered around them.

For in the dangerous game of court politics, there were no guarantees, no certainties. Only the cold, hard truth that power was fleeting, and loyalty, a rare and precious commodity.

And as Eliza watched Anne battle against the tide, she could only hope that Anne's strength, her courage, would be enough to see her through

Chapter Fourteen: The Queen's Despair

The news of Henry's hunting accident sent shockwaves through the court. Eliza was in Anne's private chambers when the messenger burst in, his face pale and his eyes wide with fear.

"Your Majesty, the King—" he stammered, struggling to catch his breath. "The King has had an accident. A fall while hunting. He is gravely injured."

Anne's face blanched, the color draining from her cheeks as she clutched the arm of her chair. "What do you mean, 'gravely injured'?" she demanded, her voice trembling.

"He was thrown from his horse," the messenger explained, his words tumbling out in a rush. "He struck his head. The physicians are with him now."

For a moment, there was only silence. Eliza watched as Anne's hand flew to her stomach, her face contorted in a mixture of fear and pain.

"I must go to him," Anne whispered, pushing herself to her feet. But as she took a step forward, she stumbled, her face twisting in agony.

"Anne!" Eliza cried, rushing to her side. "You must be careful—"

"No, I have to see him," Anne insisted, her voice strained. "I have to be there."

But as she took another step, she gasped, clutching her belly. A dark stain spread across the front of her gown, and Eliza felt her heart drop into her stomach.

"Help! Someone get help!" Eliza shouted, her voice echoing through the chamber.

The next moments were a blur of chaos. Anne was lowered onto a chaise, her face pale and drenched with sweat. Her ladies rushed in, their faces masks of horror as they took in the sight before them.

"It's too soon," Anne murmured, her voice faint, her eyes wide with panic. "It's too soon—"

"Try to stay calm, Anne," Eliza urged, her own heart pounding in her chest. "Breathe. Just breathe."

But Anne's body was wracked with pain, her breaths coming in short, desperate gasps. She clutched Eliza,s hand, her grip painfully tight, her eyes wild with fear.

"I can't lose him, Eliza," she sobbed. "I can't lose him and the baby. Please, God, don't take them both."

Eliza felt tears sting her eyes as she held Anne's hand, her own heart breaking with every anguished cry that escaped her dear friend's lips. "Stay with me, Anne. You're strong. You can get through this."

The hours that followed were a nightmare. Anne's labour was fierce and relentless, her cries of pain echoing through the chamber. Eliza stayed by her side, offering what comfort she could, though she felt utterly helpless in the face of Anne,s suffering.

Finally, as the dawn light began to creep through the windows, there was a sudden, terrible silence. The midwife, her hands stained with blood, turned to Anne, her face stricken.

"I am sorry, Your Majesty," she said quietly. "The child is gone."

Anne's scream was a sound of pure, unbridled agony, a cry that seemed to shake the very walls of the chamber. Eliza felt her own heart shatter at the sight of her friend,broken and bleeding,her hopes dashed in the cruellest way imaginable.

"No!" Anne sobbed, her body convulsing with grief. "No,not again. Please,God,not again!"

Eliza knelt beside her, her own tears flowing freely. "I am so sorry, Anne. I am so,so sorry." Her books had told her everything about this heartbreaking moment, but to be here in the room witnessing everything was absolutely heartbreaking and overwhelming and Eliza was genuinely upset at the loss of this most wanted baby.

Anne turned her face away, her shoulders shaking with silent sobs. Eliza could do nothing, but hold her hand, offering what little comfort she could in the face of such overwhelming despair.

The news of the miscarriage spread through the court like wildfire, casting a pall of sorrow and fear over everything.

Henry, still recovering from his accident, was told of the tragedy as soon as he regained consciousness.

His reaction was one of cold, stunned silence. Eliza, who had been summoned to his chambers, watched as the news seemed to sink in, his face pale and drawn.

"A son," he murmured, his voice hollow. "It was a son, wasn't it?"

"We don't know for certain,but yes I heard the midwives say it was a son,Your Majesty," Eliza replied gently. "And the Queen..She is devastated."

Henry's expression darkened, a flicker of something dangerous in his eyes. "A son,my son," he muttered, his voice low and tense. "I have lost another son."

Henry turned away, his jaw clenched. "She has failed me. She has failed me."he kept repeating, getting angry.He got up from the red velvet chair he had been sitting on and walked to the long latticed window and started shouting with his voice getting louder. One of the courtiers actually jumped, because he was so startled by the anger that had come from nowhere.

"My Mistress needs you now, more than ever," Eliza tried to say softly, so as not to anger him more. "She needs your support, your love." but the King wasn't interested Henry could not,would not face that woman today.

Eliza curtsied and left the room,and Henry was furious at the loss of a son. Anne had promised him this male child and Henry was not a man who handled loss well,and Eliza feared for what this latest tragedy might mean for Anne's already precarious position.

Eliza hesitated, her throat tight as she stood by Anne in the dim light of her chambers. The weight of what she was about to say pressed on her. How could she tell Anne the truth without revealing too much? She took a deep breath, her voice barely above a whisper.

"When… when Henry was told it was a son you lost," Eliza began, choosing her words carefully, "his anger was… overwhelming. I saw it. The way his face twisted, the way his fists clenched as if he wanted to strike the world for taking that from him." She glanced at Anne, whose eyes widened in pain.

Eliza's heart pounded as she spoke the words she had never wanted to say. "He blamed you, Anne. He spoke of curses, of the kingdom's need for a son, and how this."her words broke off.She could say no more.

Anne's breath , her hand clutching at her stomach. Eliza fought the urge to tell her everything—that she knew the future, that there was more pain to come—but she couldn't. Instead, she swallowed hard, her eyes filled with both sorrow and a helplessness she couldn't shake.

"I wish I could tell you it will get easier," Eliza added softly, her voice trembling. "But you must stay strong, for there is still so much ahead."

Anne's gaze flickered with something unreadable—a mixture of fear and resolve. Though she didn't know the depths of Eliza's knowledge, the truth lingered between them, unspoken yet unmistakable.

When Henry finally visited Anne, the encounter was fraught with tension. He stood at the foot of her bed, his face a mask of stoic control, his eyes dark and unreadable.

"I am sorry for your loss, Anne," he said stiffly, his voice lacking the warmth and comfort she so desperately needed.

Anne, her face pale and gaunt, looked up at him with eyes hollowed by grief. "Our loss, Henry," she whispered. "It is our loss."

Henry's mouth tightened, and he glanced away, his fingers flexing at his sides. "Yes, of course."

There was a long, painful silence, and then Henry turned abruptly, striding out of the room without another word. Anne watched him go, her expression shattered, and Eliza,s heart broke for her friend.

In the days that followed, Anne withdrew into herself, a shadow of the vibrant, determined woman she had once been. She spent hours alone, her face turned away from the world, her body still weak and trembling from the ordeal.

Eliza stayed close, offering quiet companionship, her heart aching for the friend she loved so dearly. But there was little she could do to ease Anne's suffering, and she felt helpless in the face of such profound sorrow.

As the weeks passed, it became clear that Henry's patience was wearing thin. His visits to Anne grew fewer, his attention increasingly focused on Jane Seymour, who seemed to hover at the edges of the court like a pale, silent ghost.

Eliza watched the king's growing infatuation with a sinking heart. She knew that Anne's position was more precarious than ever, her failure to produce a son a stain that could not easily be erased.

One afternoon, as Eliza and Anne sat together in the gardens, the sun casting dappled shadows on the grass, Anne turned to her, her eyes dark and haunted.

"I have lost everything, Eliza," she whispered, her voice breaking. "My child, my husband, my hope. What is left for me now?"

Eliza took her hand, squeezing it tightly. "You have your daughter, Anne. And you have me. You are not alone."

Anne's lips trembled, and she looked away, tears spilling down her cheeks. "But for how long? How long before he tires of me completely and casts me aside?"

Eliza,s heart ached with the truth of Anne's words,but she forced herself to smile,to be strong for her friend. "You are still the Queen, Anne. You are still the mother of his child. You have more power than you think and you must stop worrying about it all.It will make you ill."

But even as she spoke, Eliza felt a cold dread creeping into her heart. The court was a dangerous place for a woman who had lost the king's favour,and she knew that the road ahead would be fraught with peril for both of them.Eliza just knew what she had to do.

Chapter Fifteen: Fractured Hopes

The court had barely begun to recover from the shock of Anne's miscarriage when new tensions surfaced. The days seemed grayer, more somber, as if the very air was weighted with sorrow and disquiet. Eliza could sense the unease everywhere: in the servants' hushed whispers, in the stiff, guarded expressions of the courtiers, and most of all, in the strained silence between Anne and Henry.

Anne, still weakened by the loss, remained secluded in her chambers, the lively and confident Queen now a shadow of herself, her once sparkling eyes dulled with grief and fatigue.

When Mary and George Boleyn arrived at the palace, the atmosphere felt oppressive, the air heavy with the weight of unspoken sorrow. They were escorted through the winding corridors, their footsteps echoing against the cold stone floors, each step bringing them closer to the sister who needed them now more than ever.

Mary's heart ached with worry, her mind racing with thoughts of how Anne must be feeling. She remembered their childhood, when Anne was always the spirited one, the dreamer with stars in her eyes. Now, as they approached the door to Anne's private chambers, Mary could scarcely recognize the vibrant sister she had always admired.

George, his usually confident demeanor subdued, glanced at Mary, his face etched with concern. He reached out, squeezing her hand briefly before the door was opened for them by Eliza. "Whatever happens, we must be strong for her," he whispered, his voice strained.

Mary nodded, taking a deep breath as they stepped inside.

The room was dimly lit, the heavy drapes drawn against the bright winter light. Anne was seated near the fireplace, wrapped in a blanket, her gaze fixed on the flickering flames. She looked fragile, her posture hunched as if carrying an invisible burden. When she noticed them, a flicker of recognition passed over her face, followed by a weak, fleeting smile.

"Mary, George…," she murmured, her voice hoarse and weary. "You didn't have to come."

Mary rushed to her side, kneeling down and taking Anne's hands in hers. "Of course we did, Anne. You're our sister. We had to be here with you."

Anne's eyes filled with tears, and she turned her head away, as if ashamed of her own vulnerability. "I've failed everyone," she whispered. "Henry, our family… myself. I was supposed to give him a son, and now—" Her voice broke, and she covered her face with trembling hands.

George stepped forward, his expression a mixture of anger and sorrow. "Anne, you haven't failed anyone," he said firmly. "What happened is not your fault. You've been under so much pressure, more than anyone should have to bear. You've given everything for the crown, for Henry…"

"And for what?" Anne's voice rose, sharp with bitterness. She dropped her hands, revealing a face streaked with tears. "For a crown that feels like a noose around my neck? For a husband who looks at me now as if I'm nothing? All I've done is given him a daughter and disappointment." Her shoulders shook with silent sobs, her body curling in on itself.

Mary wrapped her arms around her sister, holding her tightly. "Anne, listen to me," she said softly. "You're more than just a Queen, more than just a wife. You're our sister, and we love you for who you are, not for what you can give or do. You've always been so strong, so brave. But you don't have to carry this alone."

For a moment, there was silence, broken only by the crackling of the fire. Anne leaned into Mary's embrace, her sobs subsiding slowly. George stood by, his jaw clenched, watching his sisters with a protective gaze. He felt an anger burning in his chest, not just at Henry, but at the court, at the relentless pressure that had been placed on Anne's shoulders. He wished he could do something, anything, to shield her from this pain.

A soft knock at the door interrupted the quiet moment. The siblings turned as the door opened, revealing Thomas and Elizabeth Boleyn. Anne's parents, usually so composed and proud, looked older and more weary than ever before. Elizabeth's face was pale, her eyes red-rimmed with worry, while Thomas seemed smaller somehow, his shoulders hunched as if bearing an invisible weight.

"Mother, Father…" Anne's voice was barely a whisper. She tried to rise, but Mary and George gently held her down, urging her to remain seated.

Thomas Boleyn stepped forward, his eyes filled with a pain that matched Anne's. He took her hand, his grip trembling. "Anne, my dearest child," he said softly. "You mustn't blame yourself. What happened... it is not your fault."

Anne looked up at her father, her eyes glistening with unshed tears. "But it is, Father. It is. I was supposed to give Henry a son, to secure the succession... and now I have failed." Her voice cracked with anguish, the guilt she had been carrying spilling over.

Elizabeth moved to her daughter's side, bending slightly beside her and gently cupping Anne's face in her hands. "Listen to me, Anne," she said, her voice firm but tender. "You have not failed. You have done everything you could, more than anyone could ask. You have given this family honour and pride. You have given England a future queen in Elizabeth. You are strong, Anne, stronger than you know."

Anne's tears spilled over, and she clung to her mother, her body shaking with sobs. "I feel so lost, Mother. So alone."

"You are not alone," Elizabeth whispered, stroking Anne's hair gently. "We are here. We will always be here."

Thomas cleared his throat, his voice thick with emotion. "Anne, you are our greatest pride. You have faced more than any woman should have to bear, and you have done it with grace and courage. Whatever happens, we are with you. We are your family."

The room fell silent, the family united in their shared grief and love. For a moment, the weight of the crown, the expectations of a kingdom, and the harsh judgment of the court faded away. All that remained was the bond between parents and children, a bond that, despite the pressures and ambitions that had brought them to this point, could not be broken.

As the hours passed, they talked quietly, sharing memories of happier times, of childhood games and laughter. Anne's spirits seemed to lift slightly, her face softening as she listened to George's teasing stories and Mary's gentle reassurances. Even Thomas managed a few small smiles,his usual sternness softened in the presence of his children.

But as the afternoon turned to evening, reality began to seep back in. The weight of what had happened, of what lay ahead, pressed down on them all once more. Anne looked at each of them in turn, her eyes full of gratitude and sadness.

"Thank you," she whispered. "For being here. For loving me."

Elizabeth kissed her daughter's forehead. "We will always love you, Anne."

With reluctant hearts, Mary and George stood, their time with Anne drawing to a close. Thomas and Elizabeth lingered a moment longer, their hands clasping Anne's as if they could protect her from the harsh world outside those walls.

When they finally left, Anne felt a strange mix of sorrow and strength. The pain of her loss, the uncertainty of her future, still loomed over her. But she knew she was not alone. Her family's love,their support,was a beacon of hope in the darkness.

As she lay in bed that night, the quiet of the palace surrounding her, Anne thought of her parents, her brother, and her sister. Whatever trials she would face, whatever the future held, she knew she would face it with courage. Because she was a Boleyn. And she was not alone.

The miscarriage had certainly taken a toll not only on her body but on her spirit. She looked frail and thin, her face pale and drawn. The vibrant, determined Queen who had once captivated the court now seemed distant, her eyes often vacant as she stared out the window, lost in her thoughts if she sat in a chair.

Eliza remained by her side as much as she could, offering companionship and support. But she knew that Anne's greatest need—the love and reassurance of her husband—was beyond her power to give. Henry, once so devoted and passionate, now seemed cold and indifferent, his mind and heart elsewhere.

One morning, as Eliza entered Anne's chamber, she found her sitting by the window, her hands resting on her lap, her gaze fixed on the gardens below. She didn't turn when Eliza approached, her expression distant and pensive.

"Mistress," Eliza said softly, taking a seat beside her. "How are you feeling today?"
Anne's lips curved into a faint, hollow smile. "As well as can be expected, I suppose."
Eliza hesitated, then took a deep breath. "I know this has been an incredibly difficult time for you. But you are strong,Mistress.

Stronger than anyone I've ever known."

Anne turned to look at her, her eyes dark and shadowed. "I don't feel strong, Eliza. I feel...empty. As if everything I've fought for,everything I've sacrificed,has been for nothing."

Eliza reached out,placing her hand over Anne's. "You still have Elizabeth. And you still have a chance to secure your place, to win back Henry's favour."
Anne let out a bitter laugh, her eyes glistening with unshed tears. "Henry's favour? He can barely look at me. And when he does, all I see in his eyes is disappointment. I've failed him, Eliza. I've failed to give him the son he so desperately wants."

"You haven't failed," Eliza insisted, her voice firm. "You've given him a daughter—a beautiful, healthy child. And you will have more children, I am sure of it."

Anne shook her head, her gaze returning to the gardens. "What if I don't? What if I can never give him a son? What will happen to me then?"
Eliza,s heart ached at the hopelessness in her friend's voice. She knew that Anne's fears were not unfounded. The court was rife with speculation, and there were whispers that Henry's eye had begun to wander. Jane Seymour, in particular, seemed to be the focus of much of his attention. The demure, seemingly innocent young woman from Wolf Hall in Wiltshire,was everything Anne was not: quiet, obedient, and, most importantly, untainted by the scandal that had surrounded Anne's rise to power.

"I don't know what the future holds, Anne," Eliza said quietly, even though she did. "But I do know that you are a fighter. You've faced challenges before and overcome them. You can do it again."

Anne closed her eyes, her shoulders sagging with weariness. "I wish I could believe that."

As the weeks passed, Anne's physical health began to improve, but her emotional wounds remained raw and unhealed. The court, ever fickle, had already begun to shift its loyalties. Where once Anne had been the center of attention, the beloved Queen, she now found herself increasingly isolated, her every move scrutinised and criticised .

Eliza could see the toll this was taking on her friend. Anne's temper, always volatile, had become even more unpredictable. She lashed out at her ladies-in-waiting over the smallest mistakes, her patience thin and frayed. She argued with Henry more frequently, her desperation to regain his affection driving her to say things she later regretted.

One evening, as Eliza sat with Anne in her chambers, the queen finally voiced the fears that had been eating away at her.
"He's going to leave me, isn't he?" Anne said, her voice a whisper. "He's going to cast me aside, just like he did with Katherine."
Eliza heart clenched. "You don't know that, Anne. Henry is—"
"Henry is already looking for a way out," Anne interrupted, her eyes flashing with pain and anger. "He's

found someone new, someone who can give him what I couldn't."

Eliza hesitated. She knew that rumours of Henry's interest in Jane Seymour had reached Anne's ears. But she also knew that acknowledging them would only feed Anne's despair.

"You are still the Queen," Eliza said gently. "And as long as you have Henry's child, you will always have a place in his heart."

"But will it be enough?" Anne whispered, her voice breaking. "Will Elizabeth be enough to keep me safe? To keep me here?"

Eliza had no answer to give. She could only reach out and take Anne's hand, squeezing it tightly, willing her friend to feel the strength and support she so desperately needed, As Eliza adjusted the folds of her gown, the small silver locket slipped from her pocket, landing softly on the embroidered rug beneath her feet. Anne's sharp eyes caught the glint immediately, and with a graceful bend, she retrieved it. Turning the silver locket over in her hands, a flicker of recognition crossed her face.

"I had a locket just like this once," Anne murmured, her fingers tracing the delicate engravings with a distant fondness. "I lost it years ago, at my cousin Edward's house in Salisbury in Wiltshire. He was always fascinated with strange things, always talking of the occult and forgotten knowledge. My mother scorned it, but... I listened."

Eliza's breath caught in her throat. Her pulse quickened, each beat a reminder of the impossibility of this moment. She forced herself to meet Anne's gaze, her own heart pounding with the weight of the secret she could not yet reveal.

Anne's brow furrowed as she studied the locket more closely. "The oddest thing is... I never saw it again after that visit. My cousin was always one for strange trinkets and tales, though." She paused, narrowing her eyes in thought. "How did this come to you?"

Eliza's jaw tightened, struggling to find the words as her mind whirled. She couldn't speak the truth—not yet.Eliza hesitated, feeling the weight of the moment press down on her. Her mind raced, knowing she couldn't tell Anne the full truth. Not now. But Anne's curious gaze demanded something.

"I... I found it among some old manuscripts," Eliza finally said, her voice steady, though her pulse was anything but. "I was doing some research and it appeared... almost as if it was waiting for me."

Anne studied her for a long moment, the locket still resting in her hand. "Waiting for you?" she repeated, her voice soft, curious, but with an edge of something deeper—suspicion perhaps.

Eliza nodded, forcing herself to hold Anne's gaze. "I know it sounds strange, but I can't explain it. I felt drawn to it... as if it was meant to find me. And now, here we are."

Anne looked down at the locket again, her fingers absently tracing the engravings. "Curious," she whispered, her eyes flicking back up to meet Eliza's. "This world holds so many mysteries. Perhaps we are not meant to understand them all."

Eliza swallowed hard, relieved that Anne hadn't pressed further, yet still haunted by the truth she had to keep hidden.

The summer months brought a change in the atmosphere at court. Henry, recovered from his accident, threw himself into his duties with renewed vigor. He hosted lavish banquets, attended tournaments, and spent long hours with his council, discussing matters of state but his accident had changed him.He lashed out at courtiers.Some were even put in the Tower.of London for speaking to the King about some matter he did not want to speak about.

His whole demeanour had changed and his interactions with Anne remained completely strained, their conversations stilted and formal.

Anne, for her part, tried to regain her footing. She attended every event, every function, her head held high, her smile bright and unwavering. But Eliza could see the effort it cost her, the way her hands trembled when she thought no one was looking, the way her eyes darted anxiously around the room, always searching for Henry, for a sign that he still cared.

And then, one evening, everything changed.

It was a warm, golden evening in late August. The court had gathered in the great hall for a banquet, the tables laden with food and wine, the air filled with laughter and music. Anne, dressed in a stunning gown of emerald green, sat beside Henry at the head of the table, her smile radiant but strained.

Eliza, seated further down the table, watched as the evening unfolded. She could see the tension between the King and Queen, the way Henry's gaze kept drifting away from Anne, toward the far end of the hall, where Jane Seymour sat with her family.

Eliza,s heart sank. She had hoped—prayed—that Henry's interest in Jane was nothing more than a fleeting distraction even though she knew the true story from her history books, but it was being here and witnessing everything unfolding before her very eyes and she could do nothing about it. But the look in his eyes told her anyway. There was a hunger there, a longing that she had seen before, in the early days of his courtship with Anne. As the evening wore on, Eliza found herself growing increasingly uneasy. The courtiers were watching Henry and Anne closely, their eyes bright with curiosity and speculation. And then, as the minstrel's struck up a lively tune, Henry pushed back his chair and rose to his feet.

"I would like to dance," he announced, his voice carrying across the hall.
Anne's face lit up, a hopeful smile curving her lips. "I would be honoured, Your Majesty."

But Henry shook his head. "Not with you, Anne."

The words fell like a stone into a still pond, the ripples spreading outward, leaving a stunned silence in their wake. Anne's smile faltered, confusion and hurt flashing across her face.

"Who then,My Lord ?" she asked, her voice trembling ever so slightly.

Henry's gaze shifted to Jane Seymour, who sat with her hands folded demurely in her lap, her head bowed. "Mistress Seymour, will you do me the honour ?"

A murmur ran through the hall as Jane rose to her feet, her cheeks flushing pink. She curtsied deeply, her eyes shyly meeting Henry's. "It would be my pleasure, Your Majesty."

As Henry led Jane to the centre of the hall, the minstrels struck up a new tune, a slow, graceful pavane. The King and his chosen partner began to move, their steps perfectly in sync, their movements elegant and fluid.

Eliza glanced at Anne, her heart aching at the sight of the queen's stricken expression. Anne's hands were clenched tightly in her lap, her knuckles white, her eyes fixed on the dancing couple. There was a raw, desperate pain in her gaze, a pain that cut Eliza to the core.

The dance seemed to go on forever, each step a cruel reminder of the shifting tides at court, of Henry's waning affection. When it finally ended, and Henry led Jane back to her seat, the hall erupted in applause.

Henry returned to his seat beside Anne, his expression cool and indifferent. Anne, her face pale and tight, turned to him, her voice low and strained.

"Why are you doing this, Henry? Why are you humiliating me in front of the entire court?"

Henry's eyes narrowed, a dangerous glint flashing in their depths. "You forget yourself, madam. I am the King. I will dance with whom I please."

Anne's lips trembled, her eyes filling with tears. "I am your wife."

"You are my wife," Henry agreed, his tone cold. "But you have failed in your duty. You have failed to give me a son."

The words hung in the air, heavy and unforgiving. Eliza felt a surge of anger on Anne's behalf, her hands clenching into fists beneath the table.

Chapter Sixteen: The Queen's Confrontation

The days following Henry's public slight were filled with a tense, simmering anger that seemed to radiate from Anne's very being. Word of the king's preference for Jane Seymour spread like wildfire through the court, and although many were careful to keep their voices down and their opinions muted in Anne's presence, Eliza could see the smug satisfaction in their eyes. For those who had never accepted Anne as Queen, who still whispered of Katherine and the true princess Mary, this was the beginning of Anne's undoing.

Anne, however, was not one to go quietly. The miscarriage, Henry's coldness, and the court's shifting loyalties had only fueled her determination. She was not about to let herself be discarded, like Katherine had been. She would fight, and if she was to fall, she would do so with all the fire and fury that had defined her rise to power.

One morning, as Eliza was helping Anne dress, the Queen,s anger seemed to bubble to the surface. Anne's movements were sharp and impatient, her expression tight with barely restrained rage.

"Have you seen her, Eliza?" Anne's voice was low, vibrating with intensity. "Have you seen how she parades around the court, all simpering and demure, as if butter wouldn't melt in her mouth?"

Eliza paused, meeting Anne's gaze in the mirror. "I have seen her, yes. But you must be careful, Anne. If you confront her openly, it will only play into her hands. She thrives on being seen as the innocent victim."

"Innocent!" Anne spat, her eyes flashing. "There is nothing innocent about that woman. She is a viper, lying in wait, ready to strike the moment I show any weakness."

Eliza placed a hand on Anne's shoulder, squeezing gently. "Then do not show her any weakness. Rise above it, as you always have."

But Anne shook her head, her expression fierce. "No, Eliza. This has gone on long enough. I have been patient, I have tried to ignore her, but she will not stop until she has taken everything from me. I will not let that happen."

Later that day, Eliza followed Anne as she made her way through the Palace. Anne's stride was purposeful, her head held high, her gaze fixed straight ahead. The courtiers stepped aside as she passed, their eyes widening as they took in the stormy expression on her face.

They found Jane Seymour in one of the palace's lesser-used galleries, surrounded by a few of her family members and ladies-in-waiting. The conversation halted abruptly as Anne swept into the room, her presence commanding and unmistakable. Jane turned, her pale blue eyes widening in surprise as she saw the queen bearing down on her.

"Your Majesty," Jane said, dropping into a deep curtsy, her voice soft and deferential.

"Rise, Mistress Seymour," Anne said coldly, her gaze fixed on Jane with an intensity that made even Eliza shiver. "I would have words with you."

Jane straightened, her hands clasped demurely in front of her, her head bowed in what appeared to be submission. "Of course, Your Majesty. How may I serve you?"

Anne took a step closer, her eyes narrowing. "You may serve me by ceasing this charade, by ceasing to throw yourself at the King with such shamelessness. You may serve me by remembering your place."
Jane blinked, her expression one of perfect innocence. "I do not understand, Your Majesty. I have done nothing, but show respect and loyalty to you and His Majesty."

"Do not lie to me," Anne snapped, her voice sharp as a blade. "I see what you are doing. You think you can usurp me, that you can worm your way into the King,s heart and take my place. But you will find that I am not so easily disposed of."

Jane's cheeks flushed a delicate pink, and she lowered her gaze, her voice barely above a whisper. "I would never dream of such a thing, Your Majesty. I have the utmost respect for you and your position."

"Respect?" Anne's laugh was harsh and humorless. "Is that what you call following the King around like a lovesick puppy? Is that what you call throwing yourself in his path at every opportunity, fluttering your lashes and simpering like some helpless, innocent maid?"

Jane's eyes filled with tears, her lips trembling. "I—I have only ever acted with the utmost propriety, Your Majesty. If I have given any offense, I beg your forgiveness."

Eliza watched, her heart pounding in her chest. She knew that this display of tears and contrition would only infuriate Anne further, and she was right. Anne's face darkened, her hands clenching into fists at her sides.

"Forgiveness?" Anne's voice was low and dangerous. "Do you think I am a fool, Jane? Do you think I cannot see what you are doing? You are trying to turn the King against me, to drive a wedge between us. But I warn you, do not mistake his current infatuation for love. He will tire of you, as he has tired of so many before."

Jane's tears spilled over, her shoulders shaking with what appeared to be sobs. "Your Majesty, I swear, I have done nothing to encourage the King,s attentions. I am merely a humble servant, devoted to serving you and His Majesty in whatever way I can."

Anne's jaw tightened, and for a moment, Eliza thought she might strike Jane, so fierce was the fury in her eyes. But then Anne took a deep breath, her shoulders straightening as she struggled to regain her composure.

"You play your part well, Jane," Anne said, her voice cold and disdainful. "But remember this: I am the Queen. I am the mother of the king's heir. And I will not be so easily set aside."

With that, she turned on her heel and swept out of the room, her head held high, her skirts swirling around her like a storm. Eliza followed, casting a quick glance back at Jane, who had sunk into a chair, her face buried in her hands, her ladies fluttering around her like nervous birds.

As they made their way back to Anne's chambers, Eliza could see the tension in Anne's posture, the way her hands trembled slightly as she walked. She was furious, but beneath that fury was a deep, aching fear—a fear that Eliza understood all too well.

"You were right, Eliza," Anne said suddenly, her voice tight and strained. "I should not have confronted her like that. It will only make me look like the villain, like the jealous wife lashing out at the innocent maid."

"Perhaps," Eliza agreed softly. "But you needed to say it, Mistress. You needed to show her that you will not be pushed aside without a fight."

Anne's lips pressed into a thin line. "Yes, but what good will it do? Henry will only see her tears, her supposed innocence. He will see me as the shrew, the nasty woman who cannot control her temper."

Eliza hesitated, then placed a gentle hand on Anne's arm. "Henry's feelings may be fickle, but he is not entirely blind to what is happening around him. You must be strong, Anne, but you must also be wise. You must show him that you are the Queen, that you are the one best suited to stand by his side."

Anne's eyes met hers, and Eliza was struck by the depth of pain and fear she saw there. "And if he does not see that? If he chooses her?"

"Then you must hold your head high," Eliza said quietly. "And remember that you are still the mother of his child, that you have done more than any other woman in this court to secure his legacy."

Anne's shoulders sagged, the fight draining out of her. "I am so tired, Eliza. So tired of fighting, of struggling for every scrap of affection, of respect. I thought—I thought once I was Queen, once I had given him a child, it would be enough."

Eliza,s heart ached for her friend, for the woman who had sacrificed so much, who had fought so hard to rise to the heights she now occupied, only to find those heights precarious and unstable. "You are enough,Mistress" she said softly. "You are enough, just as you are. And no matter what happens, no one can take that away from you."

Anne's eyes filled with tears, and she reached out, taking Eliza,s hand in hers. "Thank you," she whispered, her voice breaking. "Thank you for being here, for standing by me, when so many others have turned away."

Eliza squeezed her hand, her own eyes stinging with unshed tears. "I will always stand by you,Mistress .No matter what."

They sat together in silence for a long time, the weight of Anne's fears and Eliza,s helplessness heavy between them. Outside, the sun began to set, casting a warm, golden glow over the palace grounds. But inside, the shadows seemed to grow deeper, the air thick with the unspoken knowledge that the storm gathering over Anne's head was far from over.

And Eliza could not shake the terrible, gnawing fear that, no matter how fierce Anne's spirit, no matter how strong her will, this was a battle she could not win.

Chapter Seventeen: The Court's Shifting Sands

The days following Anne's confrontation with Jane Seymour were fraught with tension. The court was abuzz with whispers and rumours, and everywhere Eliza went, she could hear the murmurs of the courtiers, speculating on what would happen next. The mood was uneasy, as if everyone was holding their breath, waiting for the next dramatic turn in this unfolding saga.
Anne, though outwardly composed, was a woman under siege. She threw herself into her duties as Queen with a fervour that bordered on desperation, attending to matters of state, presiding over court functions, and engaging in endless rounds of charity work. She met with Ambassadors, and even hosted elaborate banquets, all with the hope of demonstrating her worth and securing her position.

But underneath this relentless activity, Eliza could see the cracks forming. Anne's smiles were brittle, her laughter forced, and there were moments when, behind closed doors, she would break down, weeping with frustration and fear. Her relationship with Henry was strained; he was distant, often absent, and when he was present, his gaze would stray too often to Jane, whose soft-spoken presence seemed to infuriate Anne all the more.

Eliza felt helpless, watching her friend struggle against forces that seemed determined to destroy her. She tried to be there for Anne, offering comfort and support where she could, but she knew that there was little she could do to change the King,s heart or the course of events that were rapidly unfolding.

One afternoon, Eliza was summoned to the Queen,s chambers, where she found Anne pacing restlessly, her face pale and drawn. The normally elegant room, filled with rich tapestries and lavish furnishings, seemed to have taken on a tense, oppressive atmosphere.

"Eliza," Anne said, her voice tight with urgency as she turned to face her, "I have been thinking. I cannot sit idly by and let that woman take everything I have fought for. There must be something I can do."

Eliza hesitated, unsure of what to say. "Mistress, I understand your frustration, but you must be careful."The Kings affections are fickle, and if you push too hard—"

Anne cut her off, shaking her head. "I am not talking about pushing Henry. I know that would be foolish. But there are other ways to remind him of who I am, of what I have done for him and this country."

Eliza frowned, trying to follow Anne's line of thought. "What do you mean?"

Anne stopped pacing, her eyes gleaming with a determined light. "I need to show the court that I am still strong, still the Queen they respect and fear. If I can do that, if I can rally support, then perhaps Henry will see sense. Perhaps he will remember why he loved me, why he defied the Pope and the whole of Christendom to make me his wife."

Eliza nodded slowly. "That makes sense. But how do you intend to do that?"

Anne's lips curved into a small, secretive smile. "There is to be a grand tournament in honor of Saint George's Day. All the nobility will be there, including the King. It will be the perfect opportunity to remind everyone of my place, of my power."

Eliza,s heart sank at the mention of the tournament. The jousts and displays of martial prowess were always tense affairs, where rivalries and ambitions played out under the guise of chivalric honor. They were dangerous ground, both politically and personally.

"Mistress, are you sure that is wise?" she asked cautiously. "The court will be full of people eager to see you falter, to see any sign of weakness."

Anne's smile faded, and for a moment, she looked almost vulnerable. "I know, Eliza. But I have no choice. I must show them that I am still a force to be reckoned with. If I do not, they will think I am finished, that I am nothing more than a footnote in Henry's story."

Eliza took a deep breath, then nodded. "Then I will help you in any way I can."

Anne's expression softened, and she reached out, squeezing Eliza,s hand. "Thank you. I do not know what I would do without you."

The day of the tournament dawned bright and clear, the sky a brilliant blue unmarred by clouds. Eliza accompanied Anne to the tiltyard, where the stands were filled with spectators, the air alive with excitement and anticipation. The field itself was a riot of colour, with banners and pennants fluttering in the breeze, knights in shining armour, and squires bustling about, preparing for the events to come.

Anne was resplendent in a gown of deep emerald green, the color chosen deliberately to symbolise hope and renewal. Her hair was adorned with pearls and emeralds by Eliza, and she wore a diadem that glittered in the sunlight, its intricate design framing her face like a halo. She looked every inch the Queen, her demeanour calm and regal as she took her place in the royal box beside Henry.

The King himself was dressed in the rich crimson and gold of the House of Tudor, his expression impassive as he surveyed the scene before him. Jane Seymour, seated slightly behind him with the other ladies of the court, was a picture of modesty in a pale blue gown, her eyes downcast, her hands folded demurely in her lap.

As the tournament began, the crowd cheered and shouted, their enthusiasm rising with each clash of lances, each display of skill and bravery. Eliza watched as the knights competed fiercely, each hoping to catch the king's eye, to win glory and favour But her attention was focused on Anne, who sat beside Henry,her posture straight,her gaze never wavering.

Anne's strategy soon became clear. As the tournament progressed, she made a point of praising each knight who performed well, her voice carrying clearly over the noise of the crowd. She spoke of their bravery, their skill, their loyalty to the crown, and as she did, she subtly wove in references to Henry's own qualities, reminding the spectators of the king's greatness and the role she had played in supporting him.

Eliza could see the effect this had on those around them. The courtiers, who had been watching Anne with wary, critical eyes, began to soften, their expressions becoming more respectful, more admiring. Even Henry, who had seemed distracted and distant at the start of the day, began to respond, his gaze flickering to Anne with something like approval.

But it was not just words that Anne used to her advantage. During the breaks between the jousts, she moved through the crowd with a confident grace, speaking with the nobles, the Ambassadors, even the foreign visitors who had come to witness the spectacle. She charmed them with her wit, impressed them with her knowledge of politics and diplomacy, and by the time the final joust was announced, it was clear that she had made a powerful impression.

The climax of the tournament came when a young knight, one of Henry's favourites, won the final tilt, unseating his opponent with a skillful, daring strike. The crowd erupted in cheers, and as the knight rode up to the royal box to receive his prize, Anne stood, holding out a silk favour—a token of her esteem.

"Sir Francis," she said, her voice ringing out over the din, "you have shown great courage and skill today. It is fitting that you, who have served His Majesty with such loyalty, should be honoured for your deeds."

The knight bowed low, his face flushed with pride. "Your Majesty is too kind. It is an honour to serve such a noble and gracious Queen."

Anne smiled, then turned to Henry, her eyes shining with a mixture of pride and challenge. "And now,My Lord, I believe it is your turn to show the court the true prowess of the House of Tudor."

Henry's eyes widened, and for a moment, Eliza thought he might refuse. But then he smiled, a slow, almost reluctant smile, and nodded. "Very well,My Lady. If you wish it, I shall oblige."

The crowd roared its approval as Henry rose and made his way to the lists. He donned his armour, the gleaming steel adorned with the royal arms, and mounted his horse, his movements confident and assured. As he took his position, Anne leaned forward, her hands clasped tightly together, her gaze fixed on him with an intensity that made Eliza,s heart ache.

The joust was spectacular. Henry, despite his growing girth and age, proved that he still possessed the strength and skill that had once made him the finest knight in England. He rode with power and precision, his lance striking true, his opponent sent crashing to the ground in a shower of splintered wood.

The crowd went wild, shouting and cheering, their admiration for their King rekindled. Henry, his face flushed with triumph, turned his horse toward the royal box, his eyes meeting Anne's. For a moment, there was a spark between them, a flicker of the passion and admiration that had once defined their relationship.

Anne rose, clapping her hands, her smile radiant. "My Lord, you have shown us all the true might of our King. We are blessed indeed to have such a sovereign."

Henry bowed his head, a smile tugging at his lips. "And I am blessed to have such a Queen

The words were simple, almost perfunctory, but they held a weight that was not lost on those watching. It was a small victory, a fragile, uncertain truce, but in that moment, it felt like hope.

As the tournament came to an end and the court began to disperse, Eliza felt a surge of relief. Anne had succeeded, at least for now. She had reminded Henry, and everyone else,of her strength,her charisma and her determination to fight to keep her crown

Chapter Eighteen: The King's Ultimatum

The court was abuzz with excitement in the days following the tournament, where Henry's prowess had rekindled a sense of unity among his supporters. Yet beneath this facade, the tension between Anne and Henry simmered, stoked by the increasingly prominent presence of Jane Seymour. Eliza felt the atmosphere shifting, a delicate balance teetering on the edge of upheaval.

One afternoon, Eliza entered Anne's private chambers to find her pacing restlessly, her expression a tempest of anxiety and anger. The normally vibrant space felt stifled, burdened by unspoken fears.

"Eliza, I cannot endure this any longer!" Anne exclaimed, her voice a mix of frustration and desperation. "Jane Seymour is everywhere! It's as if she's trying to eclipse me."

Eliza stepped closer, sensing the crack in Anne's facade. "You are still the queen, Anne. Your position is strong; you cannot let her undermine your power."

Anne's eyes flashed with defiance. "But Henry is drawn to her! Every day, I feel him slipping away, and it terrifies me."

Eliza took a steadying breath, knowing the precariousness of their situation. "You must remind him of your worth. You've fought too hard to let anyone diminish your standing now."

For a moment, Anne paused, contemplating Eliza,s words. "I will not let them push me aside. I have sacrificed too much for this crown."

Before Eliza could respond, Lady Rochford entered, her expression grave. "Your Majesty, the king requests your presence in the council chamber."

Anne stiffened, a flicker of apprehension crossing her face. "What does he want?"

"Something of great importance, I believe," Lady Rochford replied cautiously.

Anne straightened, her determination returning. "Very well. I shall attend him."

Eliza followed closely behind, her heart racing as they entered the council chamber. Henry stood before his advisors, his expression a mix of authority and something darker. The tension in the room was palpable.

"Your Majesty," Henry began, his voice steady but laced with an edge. "I have called you here to discuss our future."

Anne met his gaze, a mix of hope and trepidation in her eyes. "What is it, my Lord?"

Henry took a deep breath, his demeanour serious. "I am aware of the whispers that have grown louder concerning our marriage. Some suggest it is time to reevaluate our positions, to consider what is best for the crown."

Anne's heart raced, alarm bells ringing in her mind. "You cannot mean that!" she exclaimed, stepping forward. "Our marriage is solid; I have borne you a daughter. I have stood by your side through everything."

Henry's gaze was unwavering. "And yet, the court's eyes are on us, scrutinising every move we make. I cannot allow distractions to jeopardise the stability of the realm."

"Stability?" Anne echoed, incredulity lacing her tone. "You speak of stability while allowing that woman to encroach upon our lives? This is not about stability; this is about your desire to appease those who would see me gone!"

Henry's expression hardened. "This is not a matter of desire, Anne. I must think of the future. Our enemies gather; they will seize upon any weakness."

"Do you think I am weak?" Anne shot back, her voice rising. "I have fought for this crown, for our daughter! I will not be dismissed so easily."

"Then prove it," Henry replied, his tone shifting to challenge. "Show the court that you are still the Queen they should respect. Make them see that your position is unshakeable."

Eliza watched as the confrontation escalated, her heart racing. She could feel the tension crackling in the air, knowing that the stakes were higher than ever.

Anne's composure wavered, a flash of vulnerability crossing her face. "What do you wish me to do, Henry? Perform a grand display to win back your favour ? I have done everything for you, yet you still doubt my loyalty."

"Doubt?" Henry scoffed, frustration evident. "It is not doubt; it is strategy. We must navigate the treacherous waters of the court together."

The weight of his words hung heavy, a reminder that their fates were inextricably tied to the whims of the court.

Anne's eyes hardened, the fire within her reigniting. "I will not be a pawn in this game, Henry. I am your wife and the mother of your child. I deserve to be treated with respect."

Henry's expression softened for a brief moment, but the resolve in his eyes remained. "Then act like it. Show them that you are strong, that you will not be cowed by whispers."

"I will do what I must," Anne replied, her voice steady. "But know this: I will not relinquish my power without a fight. Elizabeth will not be a pawn in your schemes."

As the tension in the room thickened, Henry nodded, the conversation seemingly concluded, but Eliza could sense the undercurrents of unresolved conflict. Anne had made her position clear, yet the spectre of Jane Seymour lingered, an uninvited guest at their table.

As they left the council chamber, Eliza walked beside Anne, her heart heavy with concern. "You handled that well, but we need to be cautious. Henry may not be as steadfast as you believe."

Anne's jaw tightened, her expression fierce. "I refuse to live in fear of what others think. If Henry wants a show of strength, then he will have it. I will fight for my place in this court."

Eliza nodded, inspired by Anne's resolve, but a sense of foreboding clung to her. The challenges ahead were daunting, and the court was a treacherous landscape where allegiances shifted like the wind.

"Together, we will navigate this," Eliza vowed, a quiet determination igniting within her. "We'll ensure that Elizabeth's future is secure, no matter what it takes."

As they walked through the corridors of Hampton Court, Eliza knew that they were at the precipice of something monumental. The battle for Anne's legacy had only just begun, and they would face whatever came next with courage and unwavering loyalty.

Chapter Nineteen: Shadows Gather at Court

The air in Anne Boleyn's chambers felt heavy, laden with unspoken fears and the creeping scent of betrayal that haunted the Tudor court.

She stood near the window, framed by the soft glow of the setting sun. Her hands gripped the sill tightly, knuckles pale, as her eyes followed the figure of Jane Seymour in the courtyard below. Jane moved like a shadow, her presence quiet yet insistent, growing ever closer to the King. The murmurings of the court were beginning to poison the air Anne breathed, each glance and whisper a dagger aimed at her.

Anne's heart pounded with an ache she had grown all too familiar with—fear, not only for herself but for the kingdom she had hoped to shape. The world around her was crumbling, and yet, her regal demeanor held fast, refusing to show weakness. She turned from the window, her eyes dark and unreadable as she surveyed her chambers. The tapestries of courtly life seemed a cruel joke now, adorned with scenes of triumph and glory, while her own life spiraled toward ruin.

Eliza, standing quietly in the corner, watched as Anne paced the room with a restless energy. She had seen Anne in moments of quiet strength, but now, there was a crack in her facade, a vulnerability that even Anne could no longer hide. The weight of Henry's drifting affections pressed down upon her, and the growing presence of Jane Seymour in court was like a knife twisting in her side.

Eliza could feel the tension building within the room, a thick cloud of anxiety that neither woman could ignore. Anne's every gesture seemed sharper, her words laced with frustration as she spoke to herself, barely aware of Eliza's presence.

"Yorkshire," Anne muttered, her voice tight with restrained anger. She stopped pacing and faced Eliza, eyes narrowing with determination. "I'll send her to Yorkshire. She will be out of my sight, out of Henry's reach."

Eliza's stomach twisted. She knew this plan would only deepen the King's attraction to Jane. Henry had never been a man who responded well to being denied something he desired. Sending Jane away would only inflame his interest, and worse, it would give the courtiers more reason to whisper. The brewing dissatisfaction with Anne would only intensify.

Eliza hesitated before speaking, choosing her words carefully. "Mistress,sending her away… it may make the King—"

"I know!" Anne's voice cut through the room, sharp and brittle. She took a step forward, her hands trembling as she pressed them together in a futile attempt to regain control. "I know what Henry is like. But what choice do I have? Am I supposed to stand by and watch her worm her way into his heart? To let her steal everything from me?"

The crack in Anne's composure widened, and for the first time, Eliza saw the full depth of her fear. Not just fear of losing her crown, but the fear of losing her very identity— the woman who had captivated a king, who had fought so hard to become Queen, now watching helplessly as another woman threatened to take it all away.

"I will not sit idly by while she destroys me," Anne whispered, more to herself than to Eliza.

Eliza moved closer, her voice soft, but firm. "Mistress, Jane's presence is dangerous, yes, but sending her away will only fuel the King's desire. You know how he is. He will resent being denied what he wants. And more than that... there are already whispers at court."

Anne's eyes flickered with uncertainty, but pride overpowered her doubt. "Whispers," she repeated, as though the word itself was something she could dismiss. "They have always whispered about me. I have dealt with it before."

Eliza's pulse quickened. She could feel the mounting danger, not just from Jane Seymour, but from those at court who were aligning themselves with Henry's growing discontent. Thomas Cromwell, who had once been Anne's ally, was now watching her with calculating eyes, positioning himself for the next move. The rumors of adultery and treason were already beginning to circulate, faint murmurs in the dark corners of court life, but they would grow louder, more vicious, and they would consume her if nothing was done.

"Mistress" Eliza's voice faltered. She wanted so badly to tell Anne everything—the future, the path that awaited her if nothing changed. But the words lodged in her throat. She couldn't reveal the truth, not yet, not when she didn't even understand the full extent of her own role in all of this.

Instead, she reached into her pocket, her fingers brushing against the cool metal of the locket hidden there. The weight of it was reassuring and terrifying all at once. She knew what it represented—what it could mean. The locket had brought her here, across time, but it was more than just a relic of the past. It was a lifeline, a symbol of the choice that hung between them.

Could she take Anne back with her? Was it even possible? Eliza's mind raced with the thought. It had been so long since she'd touched the locket in that ancient manuscript, back at the Manor House. The words inscribed on the parchment still echoed in her mind, looping in elegant script:
 In the shadow of time's ever-turning wheel, the bearer shall pass unseen. Mark the silver with care, for it is the key to all that was and all that will be.

The locket felt warm against her skin, and for a brief moment, Eliza allowed herself to believe in the impossible. She glanced at Anne, who was still pacing, muttering plans to send Jane Seymour away.

Could I really do it? Eliza thought. Could I take her away from all this? Save her from a future that's already written?

But before she could speak, there was a knock at the door and Thomas Cromwell stood in the doorway, his expression as calculating as ever. His eyes flickered over Eliza, then settled on Anne with a cold, almost predatory gleam.

"Your Majesty," he said, his voice smooth but dangerous. "The King is in need of your counsel."

Anne stiffened, her back rigid as she turned to face him. "Is he now?" she replied, her tone dripping with disdain.

Cromwell inclined his head slightly, his lips curling into a smile that never reached his eyes. "Indeed. He has been… troubled of late. It seems certain rumours have come to his attention."

Eliza's stomach churned. Cromwell, ever the opportunist, was laying the groundwork for Anne's destruction, and she could see it in his eyes. He was waiting for her to slip, to make one mistake, and then he would pounce.

As Cromwell left the room, Anne's gaze lingered on the door, her fists clenched. "He watches everything," she whispered, more to herself than to Eliza.

Eliza took a deep breath, her heart pounding as she pulled the locket from her pocket and held it in her hand, staring at its intricate design. The silver gleamed in the dim candlelight, casting faint shadows on the walls. She turned it over in her palm, feeling the weight of its history, its power.

Anne noticed the movement, her eyes narrowing as she took a step closer. "That locket…" she murmured, her voice thick with disbelief. "It is beautiful."

Eliza froze, her fingers tightening around the locket as Anne's eyes bore into hers.

"I had a locket just like that," Anne continued, her voice trembling with a mix of nostalgia and fear. "I remember now,I lost it years ago, at my cousin's estate in Salisbury,Wiltshire.

Edward… he was always talking of strange things, the occult, secrets hidden in plain sight. How… how do you have this?"

Eliza's jaw dropped, her mind racing. She hadn't expected this. How could Anne have recognized the locket? How was it even possible?

"I... I found it," Eliza stammered, unable to look Anne in the eyes. "I told you that it was in an old manuscript I discovered in a manor house."

Anne's face paled, her lips trembling as she reached out, touching the locket gently with her fingertips. "Edward warned me... he told me there were things in this world that even Kings and Queens could not control. Is this one of those things?"

Eliza swallowed hard. She wanted to tell Anne the truth, wanted to explain everything. But how could she? How could she tell her friend that she was from another time, that she had seen the future—a future where Anne's life would end in tragedy?

Instead, Eliza took a deep breath and spoke carefully, her voice steady. "There are forces at work that we don't understand, Anne. Things beyond the power of any one person to change. But sometimes, we are given a choice. A chance to rewrite what was written."

Anne's eyes flickered with fear and hope, her fingers tightening around the locket. "What are you saying, Eliza?"

Eliza hesitated, her heart pounding in her chest. She could feel the pull of the locket, the faint pulse of its magic thrumming beneath her skin. She wanted so badly to take Anne's hand, to tell her that they could escape this nightmare together, that they could change the future.

But time was a cruel mistress, and the weight of history pressed down on them both.

"I'm saying," Eliza whispered, her voice low and trembling, "that we don't have to accept what's coming. There's a way out. A way for you to escape all of this."

Anne's eyes widened in shock, a flicker of hope sparking behind the fear. She glanced down at the locket in her hand, its cool silver surface reflecting the dim candlelight, as if it held within it the very power Eliza spoke of. Her breath quickened as she turned to face Eliza fully. "Escape?" Anne whispered, her voice barely audible. "What do you mean?"

Eliza stepped closer, feeling the weight of the moment press down on her chest. Every fibre of her being wanted to pull Anne away from this fate, to shield her from the horrors that awaited her. The very thought of seeing her friend, this woman she had come to admire and care for, led to a sharp ache in her heart.

She steadied her breath and looked into Anne's eyes. "You don't have to stay here. You don't have to endure the accusations, the lies, the cruelty of the court. The locket… it brought me here. And maybe—just maybe—it can take you with me, to another time. To a place where you won't have to live in fear."

Anne recoiled slightly, her face a mix of disbelief and awe. She shook her head slowly, trying to grasp what Eliza was saying. "Another time? What are you talking about?"

Eliza hesitated. Could she really explain it all? Could she tell Anne that she wasn't from this world, that she had come from centuries into the future? That she had already seen how Anne's story would end, with her condemned and abandoned?

"I'm not… from here," Eliza said finally, her voice thick with emotion. "I come from a time far ahead, beyond what you can imagine. The locket is… it's like a bridge between our worlds. It brought me to you. And I believe, if we try, it could take you to my world, where you could be free."

For a long, silent moment, Anne stood there, staring at Eliza as if she had spoken in another language. The Queen's lips parted, her chest rising and falling with rapid breaths. She took a step back, clutching the locket in her trembling hands, her gaze darting between Eliza's face and the small, enchanted object that now seemed to pulse with its own faint glow.

"You speak of witchcraft," Anne whispered, her voice tinged with both fascination and fear. "Of magic."

"No," Eliza shook her head firmly, though the line between history and myth had blurred in her own mind. "It's not magic. It's something else. I don't know how it works, but I do know this locket has power. Power to change things."

Anne pressed her lips together, her eyes searching Eliza's face for any sign of deception. "And what would happen if I went with you? Would I disappear? Would I cease to be in this world?"

Eliza swallowed hard. "I don't know," she admitted. "But staying here… we both know what's coming, Anne. The whispers at court, the accusations—there are forces moving against you. Cromwell is positioning himself, the King is… distracted. They'll try to bring you down. And Jane…" Eliza's words faltered, but she forced herself to continue. "Jane Seymour is gaining more of the King's favour every day. You know this. If you stay, they will destroy you."

Anne's face paled, her mouth pressing into a thin line. Her eyes glistened with unshed tears, but her pride, that iron pride that had carried her through so many battles, remained steadfast.

"Do you think me weak, Eliza?" Anne asked, her voice trembling but defiant. "Do you think I would run away from this? From them?"

Eliza's heart broke for her. "No. I think you're strong, stronger than anyone at this court. But even the strongest can't fight alone, not against all of them. I'm offering you a way to live, to escape before they take everything from you."

Anne clenched her fists, the locket still tightly held within her palm. Her eyes were dark with thought, her mind racing through the possibilities Eliza had placed before her. Escape.! Freedom.! A life beyond the walls of this treacherous court, away from Henry, away from the vultures waiting to tear her apart.

But it was also a life away from everything she had fought for. Her crown. Her daughter. Her legacy.

"No," Anne finally whispered, shaking her head as tears welled in her eyes. "I can't. My daughter—my Elizabeth. What would happen to her if I left? Would they brand her a bastard, strip her of her birthright?"

Eliza's heart ached. She had no answer to that. She knew, from history, that Elizabeth would eventually become one of England's greatest monarchs, but could she guarantee that if Anne disappeared? Could she be sure that history wouldn't change in unpredictable ways?

"I don't know," Eliza confessed, her voice barely above a whisper. "But staying here... you won't be able to protect her. Not when they come for you."

Anne's face twisted in pain, her emotions warring within her. She looked down at the locket once more, as if it held all the answers she needed. But it was just an object, and the decision rested squarely on her shoulders.

"I won't run," Anne said, her voice shaking but resolute. "I will face whatever comes. For Elizabeth's sake, I must." Eliza closed her eyes, fighting back the tears that threatened to spill. She had tried. She had done everything she could to offer Anne a way out. But Anne's fate was sealed, bound by her love for her daughter and her fierce sense of duty.

Silence stretched between them, thick with the weight of unspoken fears and impossible choices. Eliza wanted to scream, to tell Anne that she didn't have to be a martyr, that there was still time to change everything. But deep down, she knew that Anne wouldn't, couldn't, leave her child behind.

"I understand," Eliza whispered, her voice breaking. Anne gave a weak smile, her eyes filled with sadness. "Thank you, Eliza. For caring. For wanting to help me. But my place is here. Whatever happens... I will face it." Eliza nodded, the locket slipping from her fingers as she placed it gently on the table between them. "I'll stand by you, whatever comes."

Anne's hand rested on the locket for a moment longer, before she turned away, the weight of her decision pressing down on her like a crown of thorns.

Eliza remained there, watching her friend disappear into the shadows of the fading day, knowing that despite all her efforts, history was a relentless tide, and it would carry them both to its inevitable conclusion.

Chapter Twenty:

The arrest came without warning.

It was a warm spring morning when Anne's life was turned upside down. The sun had barely risen, casting a gentle golden hue over the court, when the heavy thud of boots filled the Queen's chambers. Eliza was at Anne's side when the doors burst open, revealing The Duke of Norfolk flanked by a detachment of grim-faced guards. "Anne," Norfolk said stiffly, bowing, but his eyes betrayed no deference. "By order of the King, you are to be taken to the Tower."
Anne's breath caught in her throat, her hand flying to her chest as if she had been struck. "The Tower?" she whispered. "On what grounds?"
"Eliza," Anne's voice trembled as she turned to her, "what is this?"
Eliza's heart raced, panic coursing through her veins. She had known this moment would come, had seen it unfold in the dusty pages of history. But standing here, witnessing it in real time, she was utterly powerless to stop it.

"I... I don't know," Eliza whispered, her voice tight with fear. "This isn't right. It's too soon. None of this should be happening yet."
Norfolk stepped forward, his face impassive. "Anne, you are charged with high treason, accused of committing adultery with various courtiers. You are to be taken to the Tower of London to await trial."

Anne's face drained of colour, her eyes widening in disbelief. "Adultery? Treason? This is madness! Who dares to make such vile accusations against the Queen of England?"

"The charges have been brought by the King,"Norfolk said, his voice flat. "Anne, I must insist that you come quietly."

Anne's hand flew to her mouth, stifling a sob. For a brief moment, the room seemed to spin around her, the weight of the accusation crashing down with unbearable force. But then, with a shaky breath, she steadied herself, her shoulders straightening as she drew on every last ounce of her dignity.

"I will go," she said, her voice soft but firm. "I will go to the Tower, for I have nothing to fear. I am innocent, and God is my witness."

Eliza stood frozen, her mind reeling. This wasn't how it was supposed to happen. How had everything fallen apart so quickly? She reached for Anne's hand, her voice trembling as she spoke. "You don't have to go alone, Anne. I'm coming with you."

Anne's gaze softened as she squeezed Eliza's hand, her lips curving into a sad smile. "Thank you, my friend. But you cannot save me from this."

As the guards moved forward, Anne took one last lingering look around her chambers, her eyes resting on the small cradle where her daughter, Elizabeth, lay sleeping. The infant now aged nearly three, stirred at the commotion, her sweet face scrunching up in confusion as her nursemaid stepped forward to retrieve her.

"No," Anne whispered, her voice breaking as she rushed forward. "Please... let me hold her."

The nursemaid hesitated for a moment, then gently placed Elizabeth in Anne's arms. The Queen cradled her daughter to her chest, her eyes brimming with tears as she pressed her lips to the child's forehead. "My darling girl," Anne whispered, her voice trembling. "Forgive me. Forgive me for leaving you."

Elizabeth stirred, her small fingers reaching up to grasp a lock of Anne's hair, and Anne let out a soft sob, clutching her daughter tightly. "You will grow strong," Anne murmured. "Strong and wise. You will be a great Queen, far greater than I could ever dream to be."

Eliza stood to the side, her heart breaking as she watched the scene unfold. She knew that Anne would never see her daughter again, knew that history had already sealed the Queen's fate. But to witness it, to see the raw pain in Anne's eyes as she said goodbye to her child, was more than she could bear.

When the guards finally stepped forward to take Anne away, it felt like the world had slowed to a crawl. Anne kissed Elizabeth one last time before reluctantly handing her to the nursemaid, her hands shaking as she released her hold on the child.

"I will always love you," Anne whispered, her voice cracking. "Always."

And then, with a deep breath, she turned back to the waiting guards, her chin held high as they escorted her from the chambers. Eliza followed closely, her heart pounding in her chest as they made their way down the long corridors of the palace.

The journey to the Tower was swift and silent. Anne and Eliza were placed in a barge, the oars cutting through the dark waters of the Thames as they glided toward the ominous silhouette of the Tower of London. The wind whipped through Eliza's hair as she glanced nervously at Anne, who sat still and composed, her hands folded in her lap.

As they approached the looming structure, the barge slowed, and Eliza's stomach churned with dread. Ahead, the infamous water entrance to the Tower came into view—the stone archway that would forever be known as Traitors' Gate. The very sight of it made Eliza's blood run cold when she used to take a river cruise on the Thames in real life,but witnessing this happening to Anne in this time, was nearly more than she could bear.

The barge bumped gently against the stone steps, and the guards stepped forward to help Anne from the boat. She hesitated for a brief moment, her gaze fixed on the water lapping at the steps, before turning to Eliza with a faint, sad smile.

"I suppose this is where our journey ends," Anne said softly. "At the gates of treachery."

Eliza swallowed hard, her voice caught in her throat. "It doesn't have to be," she whispered. "You don't have to go through with this, Anne. We can still leave—together. There's still time."

Anne shook her head, her eyes filled with a sorrow that Eliza had never seen before. "No," she said quietly. "My fate was sealed the moment I put the crown on my head. There is no escaping it now."

Before Eliza could respond, Anne stepped onto the stone steps of Traitors' Gate, her footsteps echoing in the stillness of the morning air. The Tower loomed above them like a silent predator, its ancient stones steeped in the blood of those who had come before.

Eliza followed, her heart pounding with fear and frustration. She wanted to scream, to shake Anne and tell her to run. But she knew it would be useless. The pull of history was too strong, and Anne was bound to it, no matter how much Eliza wished otherwise.

As they passed through the gates and into the Tower, Eliza couldn't help but glance at the locket. It had slipped from her own pocket when Anne had noticed it earlier, and now it seemed to shimmer with an eerie significance. They walked through, following Master Kingston who had met them at the gates, until they came to the very place where Anne had stayed,just before her coronation and it made her choke up so much to see it now, in her shocked state.
Eliza helped Anne to settle in and tried to take stock of what had happened and Anne broke down in floods of tears because she had been told just before she was arrested,that her brother George had also been taken to the Tower to await trial accused of incest with Anne.
It was so overwhelming.
Anne had done nothing,except not given the King a son. All these trumped charges against everyone were appalling and it had Thomas Cromwell,s mark all over it.Wicked man that he was.

"This locket," Anne murmured,amid her tears "How did you come by it again,Eliza" repeating herself, in her despair ..I had one just like that and lost it at my cousins Manor House in Salisbury and her voice went quiet. Eliza had been too stunned to speak, her jaw dropping as Anne's words echoed in her mind. The locket had belonged to Anne, after all. Eliza was certain of it now.

And somehow, it had found its way into her hands, drawing her into Anne's life at this crucial moment. As they tried to calm down now they were in the Tower, Eliza clutched the locket in her hand, praying with all her might that it would somehow take them away,take them to a place where Anne could be safe, where history didn't have to repeat itself.
But the Tower's cold, unforgiving stones gave no answer. And as the great iron doors closed behind them, sealing Anne's fate, Eliza knew that the only thing left to do was to hope that it could.
Inside the cold, stone walls, Anne struggled to comprehend the unfolding nightmare.
Eliza and Anne sharing whispered conversations under the oppressive silence. "Anne, you must remain strong," Eliza urged, her heart breaking at the sight of her friend in despair.

"I am innocent, Eliza," Anne whispered fiercely. "But the court has already made its decision. My uncle, the Duke of Norfolk, presides over this farce of a trial. They want my head,or worse."

As the day of the trial approached, the air crackled with tension. Eliza felt powerless, knowing that the outcome was all, but predetermined. She accompanied Anne to the trial, sitting in the shadows as the charges against her were read—these trumped-up accusations of adultery with Mark Smeaton, her brother George, and other noblemen.

Anne sat in the dock, her posture regal despite the circumstances. She faced the assembled court with bravery, her voice unwavering as she pleaded her innocence. "I am a loyal wife to King Henry. I have not betrayed him, nor have I committed any crime."

But the whispers of conspiracy had already poisoned the minds of those present. Her uncle's gaze bore into her, conflicted yet resolute. The trial was a spectacle, a grim theatre where justice was a mere illusion.

As the proceedings continued, Eliza,s heart sank. Anne's courage shone through, but she could sense the tide of fate turning against her. The charges were not about truth; they were about power and control. The court had already decided.

In the end, the verdict was delivered, and Eliza could hardly breathe as the words echoed through the hall: "Guilty of treason." Anne's fate was sealed, the weight of the injustice crashing down around them.

Days passed in a haze of despair as Anne awaited her execution and the executioner coming from Calais in France, bringing his sword with him.
Her heart heavy with the knowledge that she would never see her daughter Elizabeth again. In the cold, dim light of her chamber, she found a moment of solitude to reflect.

On her final night in the Tower, Eliza stood by Anne's side, both women aware that time was slipping away. "You are the bravest woman I know," Eliza said softly, tears glistening in her eyes."You have fought valiantly." "Eliza, promise me that Elizabeth will know of my love for her," Anne whispered,her voice breaking. "Tell her that I did not falter. I stood for what I believed in."

"I promise," Eliza replied, her heart aching. "You will always be remembered.

Chapter Twenty-One: The Final Hours

The cold stone walls of the Tower seemed to close in on them, suffocating in their stillness. Darkness enveloped the room where Anne and Eliza sat, their hands clasped tightly together. Anne's once regal composure had crumbled, and now she was a woman broken by betrayal, by the cruel twist of fate that had turned her life upside down.

Anne's body shook with sobs that came in waves, her tears falling onto her lap as she struggled to comprehend the magnitude of what was happening. How had it come to this?
How could Henry,her Henry,send her to her death after everything they had been through?

"I don't understand," Anne whispered, her voice hoarse from hours of crying. "How could he believe these lies? I loved him, I gave him everything. My heart, my body, our daughter…"

Eliza squeezed Anne's hand tighter, feeling the weight of her grief pressing down on her own chest. The air inside the Tower felt heavy with history, with the souls of those who had met their end in this grim place. Whispered voices of the men who had lost their lives only days before echoed in the darkness, making the silence unbearable.

Anne's thoughts lingered on her brother George, her dearest, loyal George, who had been executed just days earlier. His face, so full of life and laughter, now gone forever because of a King who had believed others with lies that were so wicked, and George being his own brother-in-law too.

"George," Anne sobbed,her voice cracking. "My dear, brave George. They've taken him from me. They've taken everything."

Eliza's heart ached. There were no words to console her friend.
What could she say? That the history books had told her this would happen? That Anne had always been destined for this terrible fate?
No. It would have been cruel to speak the truth.

The Tower felt colder than ever, its walls like ice around them. Eliza had tried—oh, how she had tried—to change the course of events. She had held on to the hope that the locket, the mysterious object that had brought her to Anne's side, would somehow save her. But as the hours ticked by, that hope was fading.

"I should have done more," Eliza whispered, her own tears slipping down her cheeks. "I should have found a way to stop this."

Anne looked at her, eyes red and swollen, her breath ragged. "You've done more than anyone," she said softly. "You stayed by my side when the whole world abandoned me."

The truth of Anne's words stung Eliza deeply. She had been sent to Tudor England for a reason. She was sure of it now—the locket had belonged to Anne, a token from the future sent back to guide her through this hellish time. But the knowledge that she was powerless to prevent Anne's tragic end weighed heavily on her.

The night dragged on, the hours blurring together as they cried and clung to one another. The oppressive silence was occasionally broken by the muffled sounds of guards outside the chamber or the faraway cries of prisoners being dragged to their own destinies.

As dawn began to break, casting a pale light through the narrow windows, the dreaded knock came at the door. The guards entered with grim expressions, their presence signaling the arrival of the moment they had all feared.

"It's time," Master Kingston,the Constable of the Tower, said quietly, not meeting Anne's eyes.

Eliza's stomach churned. She knew what was coming. But knowing didn't make it any easier.

Anne stood, her body trembling but her chin held high. She brushed the tears from her face,attempting to regain some of the regal composure that had defined her reign as Queen. She was determined to face her death with the same grace that had once made her the most powerful woman in England.

"I will not give them the satisfaction of seeing me weak," she whispered to Eliza, though her voice wavered.

Eliza, still clutching the locket, followed close behind as Anne was led down the cold stairs of the Tower and out into the open air.
The White Tower watching as they walked by.
The scaffold loomed before them,newly built for this gruesome purpose.

Eliza's breath caught at the sight of it. The executioner stood ready, dressed in black leather, his face obscured save for his cold, emotionless eyes. He was a phantom of death, waiting to deliver the final blow. The sight of him, eerie and unnerving, made Eliza's blood run cold.

The crowd had gathered early, their faces a mixture of curiosity and excitement, as if they were spectators at some grand event rather than witnesses to the fall of a Queen. The weight of their judgment pressed down on Eliza and Anne as they walked toward the scaffold.
It was unbearable.

Anne walked with quiet dignity, each step deliberate, her head held high despite the tremor in her limbs. Eliza could barely keep her tears in check as she watched, knowing that every moment was bringing them closer to the end.

The locket hummed in her pocket, its vibrations growing stronger with every step. It was as if it were trying to speak to her, to tell her that there was still time, that there was still a way to save Anne. Eliza clung to that hope with everything she had.

When they reached the base of the scaffold, Anne turned to Eliza, her expression soft but resolute. "Remember me,Eliza," she whispered, her voice laced with sorrow but also with a strange sense of peace. "Remember me as I was,not as I will be."

Eliza's heart shattered. "I will," she whispered back,her voice breaking. "I swear I will."

Anne climbed the steps with unwavering courage, her eyes fixed straight ahead. As she turned to face the crowd, her gaze found Eliza one last time, her lips forming the silent words that would haunt Eliza forever.
"My Elizabeth"

One of Anne's ladies stepped forward, gently tying a blindfold over her eyes as she knelt on the straw-covered platform. The air was thick with tension,the crowd holding its collective breath as the executioner lifted his sword, swinging it to gain momentum.

In those last few,overwhelming moments, Eliza rubbed the locket desperately, her fingers trembling as she prayed for some miracle to take them both away from this nightmare. She closed her eyes,willing the locket to work,to save them.

Suddenly, the world around her began to shift. The walls of the Tower shimmered and blurred, the air humming with a strange energy. There was a blinding flash of light, and Eliza felt herself being pulled away,the familiar dizziness overtaking her senses.

When she opened her eyes, the world of Tudor England was gone. She was back in the study where it had all begun, the locket still clutched tightly in her hand.

But Anne was gone.

Eliza collapsed onto the floor,her body trembling as she wept. She had failed. She had come so close, but in the end, history had claimed Anne, just as it always had. And yet, as she stared down at the locket, she knew she had been sent to Tudor England for a reason. She had been there to bear witness, to remember Anne Boleyn not just as a tragic figure, but as a woman of strength, courage, and love.
Eliza wiped her tears and stood, the weight of Anne's final words echoing in her heart.
At that moment, she knew what she had to do.

Eliza remained still for a long time, the weight of her return to the modern world pressing down on her like an unbearable burden. The silence of the study was deafening compared to the raw, intense emotions she had just witnessed in the Tower. The soft ticking of the clock on the wall was the only sound, a reminder that time marched on, indifferent to the tragedies it left in its wake. The locket felt cold now in her hand, its hum gone, as though its purpose had been fulfilled. But Eliza's heart was far from at peace. She had returned, yes, but the hollowness that filled her chest was overwhelming. Anne was gone,just as history had recorded. And Eliza,despite all her efforts,had not been able to change that.

Slowly, she stood, her legs trembling as she took in the familiar surroundings of the study. The warm glow of the lamp, the smell of old books, the quiet comfort of the room,it all felt like another world, as though she were still trapped between two timelines.

For a moment, Eliza wasn't sure where she belonged anymore.

She glanced down at the desk, where her notes and manuscripts lay, untouched. The coffee she had poured before her journey was cold, forgotten. And her iphone,her phone was still sitting there, a relic from a life she now barely recognized. With a shaking hand, she picked it up, the screen lighting up with messages and notifications that seemed utterly insignificant now. None of it mattered.

Eliza sank into the chair by the desk, her mind spinning. She had witnessed the end of Anne Boleyn, a Queen who had fought so hard, who had loved so fiercely, only to be brought down by the cruelty of a man who once adored her. And for what? For power? For a son? For reasons that would never make sense to anyone who truly understood Anne's heart.

As she sat there, Eliza realised the enormity of what she had experienced. She had been there,truly there,with Anne in her final moments. She had witnessed the bravery, the pain, the injustice.

And now, it was up to her to tell that story. Not just the history, but the truth of Anne Boleyn's spirit,the woman beyond the title of Queen, beyond the court gossip and the treachery.

She looked again at the locket in her hand, its silver surface now dull in the lamplight. Eliza's fingers traced the intricate pattern, and she thought of the day she had first found it, hidden away in an old book of manuscripts. She hadn't known then what it truly was,a connection to a past long forgotten,a key to unlocking a destiny she hadn't chosen, but had embraced nonetheless.

But now…now it was time to face the future.

With renewed resolve, Eliza opened her laptop, the screen casting a pale glow over her face. She had to start writing. Not tomorrow. Not next week. Now. She needed to make sure Anne's voice was heard, not just as a tragic figure in history but as a woman who had lived, who had loved, and who had died fighting for what she believed in. Eliza's fingers hovered over the keyboard as she struggled to find the right words. How could she possibly begin to tell such a story? How could she convey the depth of Anne's strength, the injustice of her downfall? How could she capture the heartbreak she had witnessed firsthand?

She took a deep breath, her mind swirling with memories of her time in Tudor England. The sights, the sounds, the people,it all felt so close, as though if she closed her eyes, she might find herself back there, standing beside Anne as she walked to her fate.
And then, slowly, the words came.

"Anne Boleyn was more than a Queen."

Eliza typed the sentence, her hands steady now, her heart pounding with the knowledge that this was only the beginning. She would tell Anne's story, and in doing so, she would keep her promise.
The night wore on as Eliza wrote, her thoughts pouring out onto the screen in a rush of emotion and memory. She wrote of Anne's rise, her love for Henry, the birth of Elizabeth. She wrote of the court intrigue, the betrayals, the suffocating weight of expectations placed upon a woman who had dared to challenge the status quo.

But most of all, Eliza wrote of Anne's final days,the fear, the courage, the dignity with which she faced her death. She wrote about the way Anne had looked at her that morning in the Tower, the way she had whispered, "Remember me," as if she had known all along that her story was not meant to end with her execution.

Eliza lost track of time as she wrote, the words flowing faster now, her grief transforming into a fierce determination to do Anne justice. She owed her that much. After everything they had been through together, after all the love and loss, the hopes and heartbreaks, Anne deserved to be remembered not just as a Queen,but as a woman who had fought with everything she had.

And Eliza would make sure the world knew that story.

By the time the first light of dawn began to filter through the windows, Eliza's manuscript was well underway. She leaned back in her chair, exhausted but satisfied, her fingers sore from typing. The study was bathed in the soft glow of morning, the world outside waking up to a new day.

Eliza stared at the screen in front of her, the words she had written shining back at her like a beacon of hope. The locket sat beside her, silent now, but its presence a constant reminder of the journey she had taken.

Anne's story was far from over.

Eliza closed her laptop, a sense of peace washing over her for the first time since her return. She had done what she had set out to do. She had been there for Anne in her darkest hour, and now, she would ensure that Anne's legacy lived on.

As she stood and stretched, Eliza knew that her life would never be the same. The past and the present had collided in ways she could never have imagined. And while she couldn't change what had happened to Anne, she could honour her memory by sharing her story with the world. With one lingering glance at the locket before she got in her car to drive back to London, Eliza whispered, "I remember you, Anne. I always will."

Chapter twenty two : A Legacy Remembered

In the years that followed, Eliza never let go of Anne Boleyn's memory, honouring the remarkable woman whose strength and spirit had profoundly shaped her life The family in the Manor House had gifted Eliza the locket as they were so moved by the story of Anne Boleyn. Each year, on May 19th, the anniversary of Anne's execution, Eliza made a solemn pilgrimage to the Tower of London, carrying the locket in her hand. It became a ritual of remembrance, a tribute to the Queen whose story had become inseparably linked with her own.

At each visit, Eliza would always sit in the Chapel of St. Peter ad Vincula, where Anne was laid to rest, reflecting on the legacy Anne had left behind. She would lay down lilies and roses, symbols of beauty amidst sorrow, and as she stood there, quietly contemplating, she felt an unbreakable bond with Anne, as if the threads of the past and present were woven tightly together by memory and devotion.

One year, as Eliza sat in prayer within the peaceful chapel, its soft candlelight flickering gently, a wave of exhaustion washed over her. Leaning against the cool pew for support, she heard something, a whisper, a voice that seemed to drift through the stillness.

"Remember me, Eliza," it whispered, tender, but resolute. Tears welled in her eyes as she felt the comforting presence of Anne surround her,soothing her weary soul.

But soon, weakness overtook her. Feeling faint, Eliza was helped from the chapel by a priest, who quickly called an ambulance. She was taken to the hospital, where her family,her daughters and her beloved husband, William,gathered around her, filling the room with warmth and love.

For two days, Eliza lay in her hospital bed, surrounded by those dearest to her. She spoke softly of Anne, her voice filled with reverence. "I did meet her, you know," she said, a soft smile on her lips, "and she was beautiful, such a kind and lovely lady." She shared with her daughters the stories of Anne's courage, her resilience, and the deep impact the Queen had on her life. "I will never forget how Anne kissed Elizabeth the morning she was arrested," she said,her voice breaking with emotion. "She apologised to her little girl,telling her how sorry she was that she had to leave her.
It broke my heart,but it broke Anne,s heart in two."

Eliza spoke of Anne's daughter,Elizabeth,who would go on to become one of England's greatest Queens,reigning for forty-four years with wisdom and strength. "I'm so glad I was able to tell Anne that Elizabeth would grow into a magnificent Queen," she whispered, her heart full.

On the morning of the third day, a deep sense of peace washed over Eliza, as if the whispers from the chapel were now gently calling her home. Surrounded by her family, she closed her eyes one final time, allowing herself to slip into the love that enveloped her.

In that sacred moment, as Eliza's spirit departed, a connection formed with both Anne and Elizabeth, a bond that would transcend time. She knew with certainty that she would reunite with Anne, and after fifty years apart, they would walk together through the pages of history, their stories forever entwined.

Eliza's legacy, like Anne's, lived on through her daughters, who carried forward the lessons of courage, love, and resilience. As the years passed, they, too, would visit the Tower, lighting candles and sharing stories of the Queen who faced adversity with unwavering grace.

And throughout England, the name Anne Boleyn echoed through time, just as Eliza had promised her—a testament to the enduring power of the human spirit and the unbreakable bond between love and memory.

THE END.

Printed in Great Britain
by Amazon